Ireland and South Africa
Irish Government Policy in the 1980s

IRELAND AND SOUTH AFRICA

IRISH GOVERNMENT POLICY IN THE 1980s

■BRIGID LAFFAN■

320.968

A ■▓■TRÓCAIRE STUDY

Published by

TRÓCAIRE

The Catholic Agency for World Development
169 Booterstown Avenue
Blackrock
Co. Dublin
Ireland

Tel. (01) 885385

© Trocaire 1988

ISBN 1 870072 55 3

Typeset: Typeform Ltd
Printed in Ireland by Genprint Ltd

The views expressed are the author's and do not represent those of the Institute of Public Administration.

Preface

South Africa is unique among the nations of the world in having a political and economic system based entirely on race. Membership of one or other of the racial groups defined by the white minority as 'African', 'Asian', or 'Coloured', confers a status inferior to whites with correspondingly reduced political, civil, economic and social rights. 'Africans', who comprise 74% of the population are excluded entirely from national government and are denied the most basic human rights.

Opposition to apartheid within South Africa resulted in the imposition of a nationwide State of Emergency in 1986 with severe repression, draconian press censorship and continuing violence. Between September 1984 and January 1987 over 2,200 people were killed.

The international community has repeatedly stated its abhorrence of apartheid. Notwithstanding this, strong economic ties continue to exist between South Africa and its traditional trading and commercial partners in Europe and the United States. The issue of sanctions came to the fore with the imposition of the State of Emergency. Although some action was taken against South Africa, most notably in the US Anti-Apartheid Act, the EEC's September 1986 package and, here in Ireland, the ban on fruit and vegetable imports, these actions did not go far enough to convince the South African regime or opponents of apartheid that the international community was prepared to act decisively to force change in South Africa.

Apartheid is abhorrent to Christians. As Pope John Paul II said in his address to the International Court of Justice in 1985,

> For Christians and for all who believe in a Covenant, that is, in an unbreakable bond between God and man and between all human beings, no form of discrimination — in law or in fact — on the basis of race, origin, colour, sex or religion can ever be acceptable. Hence no system of apartheid or separate development will ever be acceptable as a model for the relations between peoples or races.

For Trocaire, whose mandate it is to tackle the causes of poverty and oppression and not just the symptoms, it is imperative that we condemn such a fundamentally unjust and unChristian system as apartheid and work with South Africans who are challenging this injustice. Hence our many projects in South Africa including assistance to the victims of apartheid, human rights campaigns, legal aid centres, information centres as well as health, water and nutrition programmes. Here in Ireland, as part of our development education programme we have tried since our inception to increase awareness of the iniquity of apartheid and to influence Irish official policy towards a firm and tangible stand against apartheid.

The study that follows is the most in-depth analysis of formal Irish government policy towards South Africa undertaken to date. Brigid Laffan has meticulously analysed Ireland's position in relation to apartheid at the United Nations, in the EEC and unilaterally.

Successive Irish governments over the last 25 years have stated their opposition to apartheid in forthright terms and have sought to promote international condemnation of, and action against, apartheid. The unilateral ban on fruit and vegetable imports imposed in 1986 broke with a long-standing tradition in foreign policy-making of eschewing unilateral action in favour of concerted international action.

The study sets out the avenues that are open to us as a small country to strengthen our stance and show further tangible evidence of our opposition to apartheid as a system that demeans and dehumanises the vast majority of South Africa's people.

Brian McKeown
Director
Trocaire

February 1988

Acknowledgements

I would like to thank Trocaire for asking me to undertake this study on Ireland's policy towards South Africa. Mary Sutton nurtured it from beginning to end and was exceptionally helpful. The members of Trocaire's Research Advisory Group, Alan Matthews, Patrick Commins, Connell Fanning, Damian Hannan and Eoin O'Malley, read drafts of the study and made many constructive comments. Anne Kinsella in Trocaire's library kept me up to date with new publications on South Africa and press cuttings. Fergus Mulligan gave expert help in editing the text and preparing the final version for publication. Mary Nolan and Helen Taylor provided valuable secretarial assistance. Thanks also to other members of Trocaire's staff for their comments and suggestions.

I owe a particular debt to officials in the Department of Foreign Affairs who supplied me with material, in particular copies of all of the 'explanations of votes' concerning UN votes, and commented on a draft. Officials in the Departments of Industry and Commerce, Labour, Agriculture, Health, the Central Statistics Office, the IDA, Shannon Development and the ESB made themselves available for interview or sent me material for the study. My thanks also to those politicians who gave me an insight into policy making on South Africa.

The accredited embassies of the EC states, the Scandinavian countries and the United States in Dublin sent me data on the positions of their respective governments. Special thanks are due to the director of AWEPAA, Mr Nico Scholten and members of his staff, who read an earlier draft and to Kadar and Louise Asmal who gave me access to Anti-apartheid Movement papers. Professor Patrick Keatinge brought his expertise on Irish foreign policy to bear on an early draft. Michael Mulreany of the IPA and Rafique Mottiar of the Central Bank gave me invaluable assistance on the presentation of trade statistics. Carmel Coyle of UCD acted as my research assistant and must be congratulated on her attention to detail and her cooperation from the outset.

The staff of the National Library of Ireland were very helpful in providing UN publications and the European Commission and European Parliament offices supplied copies of official EC documents; Dermot Scott gave me last minute results of EP resolutions.

Finally, my decision to undertake this study, despite the arrival of Diarmuid, owes much to the influence of my mother who tried to ensure her children never ate Outspan oranges and to Anne who lives in South Africa and hopes for the emergence there of a non-racist government.

Responsibility for the views expressed and any errors rests of course with me.

Brigid Laffan, February 1988

Contents

Tables and Figures

FIGURES

Summary and Recommendations

Chapter One: The Issues in Focus

Sets out the range of policy options available to governments to influence the South African government and reviews South Africa as an issue in Irish foreign policy.

Chapter Two: Ireland's Stance on South Africa at the United Nations

Irish politicians and diplomats have shown particular attention to the General Assembly agenda item dealing with apartheid.

The analysis of voting suggests consistency between 1980–1986. Ireland favours most apartheid resolutions. Abstention is used to register disapproval of resolutions which Ireland broadly supports but contain clauses it feels unable to endorse. Negative votes indicating strong disapproval are infrequent. On major policy issues, that period saw the use of a 'no' vote on comprehensive sanctions from 1984-86 whereas abstention was preferred before 1984 and in 1987. Ireland supports the use of selective, graduated economic instruments against South Africa.

Chapter Three: The European Community, Ireland and South Africa

The EC's South African policy evolved from declaratory diplomacy and a Code of Conduct for European firms in South Africa to limited sanctions in 1986. The negotiations were highly conflictual and tortuous because the UK, Germany and Portugal opposed sanctions. The 1986 agreement represented the lowest common denominator as it excluded coal, the most important item in the original package.

Irish Foreign Ministers and diplomats are committed to European Political Cooperation and forging consensus among Member States. EPC offers an additional arena of influence but to date the EPC consensus falls short of Ireland's preferred policy. Ireland supports an EC coal ban.

Chapter Four: The Domestic Environment and Irish Policy Towards South Africa

Ireland's economic links with South Africa are not sizeable but material interests do affect policy. Trade, especially in computers, has increased and South African investment in Shannon is an important issue for the government.

The ban on fruit and vegetable imports in March 1986 countered the policy line of the last 20 years for concerted rather than unilateral measures. The refusal of a small group of workers at Dunnes Stores' to handle South African goods was the catalyst.

Since the ban, the traditional policy line has re-emerged. Dail statements repeat that concerted action is more effective than unilateral measures.

Chapter Five: Conclusions and Policy Recommendations

Escalating violence in South Africa from 1984 led to a worldwide reassessment of policy towards that country. Since the unilateral ban on imports of South African fruit and vegetables Ireland has reverted to a policy favouring selective, graduated sanctions imposed by the UN Security Council and collective EC measures.

This study addresses 14 **Recommendations** to the Irish Government.

1. A unilateral ban on imports of **coal** from South Africa and exports of **computers** to South Africa should be considered.
2. As a prelude to further restrictive measures, a **licencing system** for all trade with South Africa should be introduced.
3. Alleged **breaches** of the spirit, if not the letter of the unilateral **ban** on fruit and vegetable imports, should be investigated urgently.
4. All future restrictive measures, whether unilateral or multilateral should include a **monitoring device**.
5. A **visa regime** for South African visitors to Ireland should be introduced.
6. **Aid to SADCC** (Southern African Development Coordination Conference) should be increased to assist the countries adjacent to South Africa to reduce their dependence on it.
7. A special fund to aid the **victims of apartheid** should be established.
8. Within the **EC** Ireland should work for agreement to ban coal **imports** from South Africa.
9. In the absence of consensus, Ireland should press for **partial agreement on coal** using parallel national measures among likeminded EC states.
10. Ireland should press for parallel measures to be imposed on **trade with Namibia.**
11. At the **UN** Ireland should continue to work with likeminded European and Third World countries to promote concerted international action in the form of **mandatory sanctions** against South Africa.
12. Ireland should use all **diplomatic channels** and **international organisations** to make its views on South Africa known, to exhort the South African Government to begin negotiations, and to promote human rights in South Africa.
13. Contact should be maintained with **opposition groups** in South Africa.
14. Within Ireland, **development education** and information campaigns about South Africa should be supported and the Government should from time to time inform organisations representing sportspeople, musicians, entertainers etc., as well as employment agencies or firms who recruit for South Africa of Irish Government policy on apartheid.

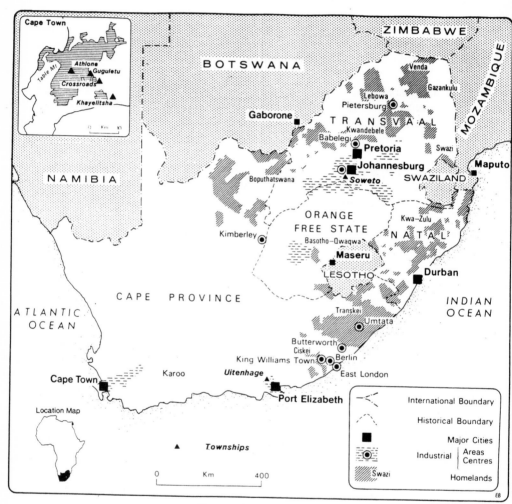

South Africa

■ CHAPTER 1 ■
The Issues in Focus

The Issues

The Republic of South Africa is a pariah state in the international system. Many governments have been condemned for violations of human rights or acts of aggression against neighbouring states but none as persistently as South Africa. Since the 1950's, the proceedings of all sorts of international fora have resounded with condemnations of South Africa and calls for the dismantling of apartheid. Apartheid or separate development antedates the National Party (Afrikaner) Government which came to power in 1948. From that date, however, apartheid was adopted as Government policy. Since then the National Party has introduced a series of laws and policies, described in the Brief History of Apartheid appended to this study, which systematically discriminate against the non-white population in all facets of life. Repressive legislation is used to contain opposition forces and to maintain white supremacy. What distinguishes South Africa from other repressive regimes is the fact that its political and economic system is now based entirely on race.

South Africa's occupation of Namibia and its policy of destabilisation in Southern Africa also invoke international condemnation. After the First World War South Africa was granted a mandate by the League of Nations to administer South West Africa (Namibia), a mandate that was revoked by the UN General Assembly in 1966. Since then South Africa has thwarted attempts by the UN to grant independence to Namibia under the terms of UN Resolution 435, 1978.[1]

In 1971, the International Court of Justice declared that the continued occupation by South Africa was illegal and that South Africa was under obligation to withdraw its administration from Namibia immediately.[2] Destabilisation of neighbouring states by South Africa has been a major factor since Mozambique and Angola gained independence in the mid 1970's. While acknowledging the importance of these issues, this study focuses primarily on apartheid and Ireland's response to it.

There has been continuous resistance by the non-white population to apartheid. This resistance has not always received the attention of the international community. Although South Africa is a perennial issue in international politics, its importance peaks at certain times. The 'conscience' of the 'international community' is usually pricked when violence and repression reach new heights. The Sharpeville massacre (1960) of 67 unarmed protestors focused international attention on South Africa. As active resistance to white rule ebbed with the imposition of the state of emergency, the agenda moved to other conflicts and regions of the world. In 1976, protests by some 20,000 Soweto school children sparked off another wave of violence.

The recent wave of black resistance began in opposition to the 1983 constitution which gave no consideration to a political role for the 25 million blacks (74% of total population) in South Africa. The extent and nature of the protest led the Government to declare a state of emergency in July 1985 in an effort to restore order. This was lifted in March 1986 only to be reimposed in June of that year. Between September 1984 and January 1987 over 2,200 people have been killed.[3]

South African Government figures show that in April 1987, 1,424 children between the ages of 12 and 18 were held in detention under emergency regulations. The real figure is higher.[4] This statistic shows, on the one hand, the extent to which children and young people in South Africa have become politicised, and on the other hand, the extent of repression. A clampdown on media reporting of the protests and the violence of the South African security forces has been used by the Government to weaken demand in the industrial countries for action against South Africa.

There is no evidence that the South African Government is willing to change the system in any fundamental way. At no stage has the Government conceded to negotiations with the leaders of the majority population. The May 1987 election strengthened the Botha government as the National Party increased its share of parliamentary seats. Support for the right wing opposition also increased; the Conservative Party became the official opposition in place of the liberal Progressive Federal Party (PFP). The minority population used the election to demonstrate support for the status quo and to reaffirm South Africa's racial policies. Intransigence and an unwillingness to entertain peaceful and meaningful change characterises the attitude of the South African Government and the sizeable majority of the white inhabitants. The conflict in South Africa poses a serious challenge to the international community. Although the fate of that country rests largely with the people of South Africa themselves, the outside world has a role to play in encouraging meaningful change and the dismantling of apartheid.

Policy Options

Governments wishing to alter or influence the behaviour of another country, in this case South Africa, have a range of options available to them. Policy instruments include diplomatic bargaining and persuasion, economic measures, sports, cultural and academic boycotts and the use of force. There is no support among the industrialised states for the use of military power as a means to get the South African Government to alter its regional and domestic policies. UN resolutions pledging support for the armed struggle being conducted by the African National Congress (ANC) do not receive support from the North American and West-European States; some do however provide humanitarian assistance to the ANC.

The purpose of this section is to provide a typology of policy instruments that have been used or may be used by Governments on the South African issue.

Diplomatic measures The whole gamut of diplomatic instruments, notably, declarations, demarches (formal diplomatic notes), withdrawal of diplomats, breaking of diplomatic relations, resolutions in inter-. national fora and so on have been used to persuade South Africa to negotiate change. When President Reagan came to office in 1981, his administration began a period of 'constructive engagement' with the Botha Government. The thinking behind 'constructive engagement' was that public criticism of apartheid should be toned down while increasing private dialogue with the South African Government as part of an effort to encourage positive change in South Africa.[5] As the situation in South Africa deteriorated from 1983 onwards and South Africa became an important issue at domestic level in the United States, the policy of 'constructive engagement' was seen not to have attained its original objectives. The passage of the US Comprehensive Anti-Apartheid Act (October 1986), signaled the end of 'constructive engagement' as the main plank of US policy.

In October 1985 the British Commonwealth, in establishing a small group of Eminent Persons in an attempt to encourage the process of political dialogue in South Africa, launched the last major diplomatic effort to get the Botha Government to negotiate change. In 1986 the group led by Mr. Malcolm Fraser, a former Prime Minister of Australia, and General Olusegun Obasanjo, former Head of Government in Nigeria visited South Africa.[6] The Eminent Persons Group published a report in June 1986. At the end of six months of meetings including 20 with the South African Government, the group concluded that 'the South African Government is not as yet prepared to negotiate fundamental change, nor to face the prospect of the end of white domination and white power in the foreseeable future'.[7] Diplomatic measures on their own have not led the National Party to the negotiating table.

Sports, cultural and academic boycotts Boycotts of this nature have featured prominently in policy initiatives against South Africa. Their purpose is to isolate the white population and to make them aware of international disapproval. They involve discouraging people from travelling to South Africa, prohibiting South Africans from attending conferences and international gatherings and exposing people who maintain links with South Africa. The UN Special Committee on Apartheid publishes a list of sports people and entertainers who go to South Africa on a regular basis. Boycotts are a means by which governments co-opt domestic groups in support of their foreign policy objectives. The main difficulty with such actions is that they cannot be enforced by national authorities . At best, Governments where possible can refuse exchequer funding to groups that maintain contact with South Africa and may refuse visas to people travelling from South Africa.

The academic boycott has been the subject of much debate because it is argued, with some justification, that the English speaking universities in South Africa are centres of opposition to the regime. By restricting contact with such academics, it is argued, the boycott defeats its own purpose. Dr Conor Cruise O'Brien accepted an invitation to visit the University of Cape Town in 1986. The visit aroused much opposition and he was eventually forced to abandon his lecture series. Although the University authorities defended his right to speak, a number of academics at the University of Cape Town, in opposing Dr O'Brien's visit, claimed that 'true academic freedom and freedom of speech are inseparable from the establishment of fully democratic institutions in a free society.'[8]

Sanctions The prohibition of trade and other economic links now dominates the debate on South Africa and are seen as a non-violent means of last resort. As early as 1960, Chief Albert Luthuli was calling for sanctions.[9] Each time the cycle of violence reaches a new peak, calls for the use of economic instruments intensify. Such calls were largely ignored by industrialised countries until the present wave of unrest. Since 1984 a wide range of sanctions have been imposed by international organisations such as the Commonwealth, the European Community, the Nordic Council, national Governments, individual national Government departments and County Councils (a list of measures is given in Appendix A). Nor have sanctions being restricted to Governments; trade unions, companies, and banks have withdrawn from South Africa or boycotted links with that country.[10]

A large variety of economic measures have been discussed in relation to South Africa notably trade sanctions, financial sanctions, disinvestment, prohibition on the transfer of technology and sanctions on services such as landing rights. Hanlon and Omond (1987)[11] list six different types of economic and financial action that could be or have been used against South Africa:
1. Total boycott
2. Ban on sales and technology transfer
3. Ban on purchases from South Africa
4. Financial bans
5. Companies' withdrawal or disinvestment
6. Other trade and economic action.

Table 1 lists the various measures which might be taken under each heading.

TABLE 1
Directory of Sanctions

1	*Total Boycott*

2.	*Ban on Sales and Technology Transfer*
2.1	Total ban on exports to South Africa
2.2	Arms
2.3	Oil
2.4	Nuclear collaboration
2.5	Computers
2.6	Other high technology/licences
2.7	Services
2.8	End export support
2.9	Regulation of trade

3.	*Ban on Purchases from South Africa*
3.1	Total ban on imports
3.2	Agricultural products
3.3	Industrial minerals and steel
3.4	Precious metals, coins, diamonds
3.5	Purchase of arms
3.6	Other industrial products

4.	*Financial Ban*
4.1	Total investment ban
4.2	Ban on new investment
4.3	Total loan ban
4.4	Prohibition of some loans
4.5	Prohibition of IMF loans to RSA

5.	*Companies*
5.1	Withdrawal
5.2	Disinvestment
5.3	Shareholder action
5.4	Boycott campaigns against companies in RSA

6.	*Other*
6.1	Selling off gold
6.2	Cutting air and sea links
6.3	Limiting travel and tourism
6.4	Ban on recruiting
6.5	Ending double taxation agreements
6.6	Ban on posts and telecommunications

Source: Compiled from Hanlon and Omond 1987, pp.300-2

1. *A total boycott:* This is the harshest possible measure that may be taken. It involves a total ban, financially, and in terms of trade with South Africa. Its purpose is the complete isolation of South Africa within the international economic system.

2. *Ban on sales and technology transfer:* Action of this kind seeks to prohibit or at least restrict export of goods and services including the transfer of technology to South Africa. In addition to a total ban, states may prohibit the sale of certain specified products, such as arms, oil, nuclear products, computers, high technology licences and end export promotion.

3. *Ban on purchases from South Africa:* The purpose of a ban on imports from South Africa is to deny that country the foreign currency it requires to purchase goods from abroad. In addition to a blanket ban on imports, countries may opt for a partial ban on various products, such as agricultural goods, industrial minerals including coal, precious metals, gold coins and diamonds, arms and other industrial products. Secondary boycotts by trade union workers have also been important in this regard as have boycotts by individual consumers.

4. *Financial ban:* Bans of this nature are intended to restrict the flow of capital to South Africa. Action may include a total ban on investment, a ban on new investment, or prohibition of loans to South Africa by commercial banks and the International Monetary Fund.

5. *Companies:* Activity here represents attempts to get private companies to reduce or to cut their links with South Africa. Since 1980 nearly 200 companies have disposed of their South African equity interests. More than half of the withdrawals however include agreements to continue to supply goods and services to South Africa. Disinvestment refers to prohibitions on investment in South Africa and withdrawal of funds from South Africa, notably, by pension funds. Boycott campaigns to force companies to leave South Africa have been especially important (Shell is at present the major target for the International Anti-Apartheid Movement).

6. *Other trade and economic action:* Action categorised under this heading includes selling off gold, cutting air and sea links with South Africa, limiting travel, tourism and a ban on post and telecommunications.

The effectiveness of sanctions is determined by the nature of the measures adopted, the vulnerability of the target country and the degree of collaboration among those countries imposing sanctions. Sanctions are more likely to be successful
— the smaller and weaker the target state is;

- the closer the ties between the initiator and the target state;
- the more precise the objectives of the initiator states: the more un-aceptable their consequences for the target state, the more fundamental the principle involved, the greater the likely resistance;
- the more realistic the assessment of what sanctions can achieve;
- the more effective and ruthless the sanctions;
- the more quickly and thoroughly sanctions are implemented;
- the lower the cost to the imposing state;
- the better the planning and the more favourable the time;
- the more watertight the boycott.[12]

On the basis of these criteria, Braun and Weiland (1987) conclude that South Africa is neither the ideal target nor an impossible target. It is heavily dependent on trade in manufactured goods with the industrialised countries.[13] Over the last number of years its economy has experienced a period of considerable turbulence. It requires loan finance from outside capital markets. On the other hand, the South African Government seems determined not to yield to outside pressure. It remains in control of the country despite four years of sustained domestic and international pressure. South Africa has had many years to plan for sanctions and to develop sanction busting strategies.

Sanctions: For and Against

Opponents of sanctions have assembled many arguments since restric-tive measures were first mooted in the 1950's.[14] Sanctions, it is claimed, are an ineffective means of bringing about political change; the use of sanctions in the past, notably against Rhodesia, is cited as an example of failure. The laager mentality of the Afrikaner, it is argued, will strengthen the resolve of the white population in the face of external pressure. The deleterious effect of sanctions on the masses of black unskilled labour, including migrant workers from neighbouring states, surfaces again and again in the debate. President Reagan, when opposing restrictive measures, stated that the US had no wish to 'punish South Africa with economic sanctions that would injure the very people we are trying to help'.[15] In a similar vein, the British Prime Minister, Margaret Thatcher said, 'Nor do I care to defend sanctions in the face of unemployment, poverty and famine among black families in South Africa where, it should be remem-bered, there is no social security welfare'.[16]

The economic dependence of the frontline states and possible retaliatory action by South Africa is another frequently cited argument. Economic interests also surface although never as directly as the question of unem-ployment among the black population in South Africa. The dependence of the industrial nations on South African supplies of a number of non-fuel minerals is raised again and again. South Africa could respond in the

21

face of escalating international sanctions by placing an embargo on the export of these products thus reducing the readiness of the industrialised countries to impose extensive sanctions. Finally, substantial job losses are forecast in the industrial countries if exports to South Africa are restricted.*

Proponents of sanctions recognise that they are unlikely to be the major agent of change nor are they perceived as an instant remedy. Moorsom (1986) argues that, in conjunction with the internal struggle, sanctions will accelerate the process of change.[17] Hanlon and Omond (1987) conclude that there is a growing acceptance that 'sanctions may not be a perfect weapon but no others are available'.[18] They highlight two overlapping strategic goals that sanctions may achieve. These are:

1. To persuade white South Africans that it is in their own interest to negotiate a prompt and peaceful handover of power to the majority population;
2. To reduce the ability of the white minority to suppress the black majority.[19]

According to these writers, sanctions could contribute to these goals by denying South Africa essential items such as arms, oil, computers and other high technology goods. By squeezing the South African economy of foreign currency sanctions would create strain within the economy and lessen its capacity to suppress the majority population. These measures would hit at white morale by imposing a 'tax on apartheid'.[20]

Proponents of sanctions raise political, moral, and economic issues in support of their cause. The behaviour of the South African Government over the last twenty years offers to many the most compelling reason for sanctions. As already stated, there is no evident willingness to alter the fundamentals of apartheid, to withdraw from Namibia or to cease aggressive acts against neighbouring states. The Eminent Persons Group concluded that

> The South African government is concerned about the adoption of effective economic measures against it. If it comes to the conclusion that it will always remain protected from such measures the process of change in South Africa is unlikely to increase in momentum and the descent into violence would be accelerated. . . . It is not whether such measures will compel change; it is already the case that their absence, and Pretoria's belief that they are not to be feared defers change.[21]

*The most recent major study questioning the usefulness of sanctions is *Sanctions and South Africa: The Dynamics of Economic Isolation* by Merle Lipton which appeared as this book was going to press. It is likely to become an important part of the debate on sanctions. Lipton suggests that sanctions have unintended and perverse effects and are often imposed with self-interest motives. They do, however, fuel the fears of disinvestment among the business community of South Africa. She envisages gradual implementation leading to a major escalation in the future. However she argues that sanctions, even full sanctions, would not produce a dramatic or quick collapse of the South African economy and would achieve no more than a process of attrition. Furthermore, she concludes that external pressure, including sanctions, have reduced what she calls the 'political space' for the opposition. There was never much 'political space' in South Africa anyway; the Botha Government has never been prepared to negotiate with the leaders of the majority population concerning their role in the political process.

As Trocaire and the Irish Commission for Justice and Peace have argued, for countries which condemn apartheid but are unwilling to support the use of force, sanctions and other restrictive measures must be considered as the only non-violent means of last resort.[22] The extensive economic ties between South Africa and the major industrial countries helped to create white privilege and to sustain it.

The attitude of the majority population and the African states bordering South Africa must be considered in any discussion of sanctions. There are very real dilemmas facing black leaders when calling for sanctions because restrictive measures will hit the black population more seriously and more readily than the white population. Nevertheless the ANC has favoured economic measures since 1960. Archbishop Desmond Tutu called for sanctions in April 1986 because the government was failing to remove apartheid. He argued that the black population 'are suffering already. To end it, we will support sanctions even if we have to take on additional suffering.'[23] Opposition groups such as the United Democratic Front (UDF) and the Azanian People's Organisation (AZAPO) have supported calls for sanctions. The leaders of the frontline states have also in recent years intensified their demand for sanctions and have used their international contacts to pressurise the industrialised countries.

Sanctions pose a particularly acute dilemma for the trade union movement in South Africa because of the implications for the employment and incomes of their members. The instinct of trade union leaders is to protect employment and wage rates. The leaders of the Congress of South African Trade Unions (COSATU) have called for disinvestment.[24]

Not all black leaders favour sanctions. Chief Buthelezi, leader of Inkatha, is a major opponent of restrictive measures and is supported by the leaders of a number of the homelands. There has been a number of surveys conducted in South Africa aimed at assessing the attitude of the majority population towards restrictive measures. The results vary widely and have been hotly debated.[25] The results of a nation-wide survey conducted in September 1985 found that a decisive majority of urban black South Africans support some form of disinvestment as a means of helping to end apartheid. The survey found that 26 percent of those questioned favoured free investment, 49 percent conditional disinvestment and 24 percent total disinvestment.[26] Orkin (1986) concludes that blacks are prepared to endure more, provided it will help unseat white oppression.[27]

Those in favour of sanctions have sought to counter the arguments against restrictive measures on a number of other grounds. It is claimed that sanctions have worked, even if not perfectly. The oil embargo forced South Africa to run up an excessive foreign debt, while anti-apartheid pressure in the US caused banks there to call in South African loans on 1 September 1985. In the ensuing economic chaos, a group of South Africa's top businessmen flew to Zambia for their first ever talks with ANC leaders. Thus the embargo contributed to the first tiny step towards talks between black and white interests.[28] Although there are numerous analyses of the effect of different kinds of sanctions the attitude of each country towards restrictive measures is moulded by the interplay of direct economic self-interest, pressure from domestic groups, the actions of allies and the nature of the debate in international organisations.[29] Assessments of the likely consequences of sanctions are used in a highly political manner.

The debate on sanctions is diffuse and highly conflictual. There is considerable argument concerning the restrictive measures that may be adopted, their effectiveness and their costs both to the target state (South Africa), neighbouring states and the states imposing sanctions. There is little consensus on the appropriate arena for sanctions – global, regional or unilateral measures. Since 1984, some countries have attempted to co-ordinate and develop a policy stance on sanctions in a host of foreign policy settings. Nor have governments necessarily been in control of the debate; the 'attentive public' has been very active in many countries and has to an extent directed the policy agenda. Governments have been compelled to impose restrictive measures sometimes against their will.

South Africa as an Issue in Irish Foreign Policy

'Like other small countries, be they neutral or members of military alliances our interests can be directly affected by events happening far from our shores.'

Peter Barry TD, Minister for Foreign Affairs, speaking in Dail Eireann, 30 May 1986.[30]

Countries pursue a variety of interests in the international system relating largely to security, economic and moral concerns. Wolfers (1962) distinguishes between 'possession goals' and 'milieu goals' in the making of foreign policy: the former refers to issues of direct national advantage and the latter to conditions in the international system such as order and justice.[31] A desire for world peace, faith in international institutions, respect for international law and human rights, and disquiet about the arms race are among the 'milieu goals' that feature in Irish foreign policy.[32] For Ireland, South Africa impinges both on direct economic concerns and ethical considerations arising from a commitment to human rights and the dignity of the individual. This study will assess the balance between economic interests and moral concerns in shaping Ireland's response to apartheid.

Ireland does not maintain full diplomatic relations with South Africa; the interests of Irish citizens in South Africa are dealt with by a consular service. Ireland has consistently condemned the policies of apartheid in international fora. Dr Garret FitzGerald, when Foreign

Minister, argued that Ireland's opposition to apartheid is in line with 'our historic position as a nation which has suffered from colonisation and various forms of discrimination'.[33]

The following statement made at the UN General Assembly (1984) captures Ireland's forthright condemnation of the South African system. Ireland's permanent representative said on that occasion:

> My government considers the policies of institutionalised racial discrimination practised by white South Africans under the name of apartheid are morally wrong. They are dangerous. They cause immense human suffering and directly contradict the fundamental values which we hold as well as the aspirations and purposes of this organisation and its charter.[34]

Irish policy has as its central objective the dismantling of apartheid although successive Irish governments have refused to condone violence as a strategy for the attainment of this objective. Irish policy aims to pressurise the South African authorities to negotiate peaceful change with the black population. This requires according to Ireland's permanent representative at the UN

> a determination on the part of the international community not to rely on exhortation alone, but also to increase significantly the pressure from outside South Africa to promote change.[35]

Ireland's opposition to apartheid did not always find expression in cool relations with South Africa. Speaking the Dail in 1959, the Taoiseach Mr. Sean Lemass, said that

> the Government entertain nothing but friendly sentiments for South Africa. Our relations, have, indeed, always been marked by mutual sympathy. However when certain policies of the Union Government, with serious moral implications have come under discussion our delegation has consistently felt obliged to record its dissent from these policies.[36]

Sympathy in Ireland towards the Afrikaner dated from the Boer War. Later during the Imperial Conferences of 1926 and 1930, Ireland in an effort to secure a definition of dominion status, enlisted the support of the other dominions. South Africa pursuing a similar goal readily lent its support which resulted in the Statutes of Westminster 1931.[37] In the aftermath of the Sharpeville Massacre (1960), Ireland's pronouncements on apartheid became considerably harsher.

Foreign policy action is the product of pressures both in the international system and the domestic arena. Multilateral diplomacy looms large in the foreign policy of small states: involvement in international organisations affords them a degree of protection and an opportunity to influence events in a world dominated by more powerful interests.[38] The UN and the EC are the two major international arenas Ireland uses for the articulation of policy. Until membership of the EC in 1973, activities

25

at the UN formed the core of Ireland's global foreign policy. Participation in European Political Cooperation (EPC) has given Irish foreign policy a strong regional dimension. The evolution of the European Community's policy towards South Africa, its links with the frontline states, and policy instruments that have been adopted by the Community are relevant. Ireland's policy both affects and is affected by the nature of the debate on this topic in the UN and the EC. Given the importance of multilateral diplomacy for Irish foreign policy, it is necessary to assess the possibilities and limits of concerted action. The following questions are considered: Has Ireland been active in shaping the agenda in these fora or has it reacted to policy initiatives and stances emerging from other countries? What kinds of coalition building with 'likeminded' states is Ireland engaged in? Has multilateral collaboration strengthened action against South Africa or has it acted as a constraint?

The third major area is the domestic context of policy. The establishment of an Anti-Apartheid movement in 1964 as a 'cause group' dedicated to the abolition of apartheid altered the domestic environment within which policy evolved. It led to the existence of an 'attentive public' on this issue.[39] Put briefly, this means that there is an organised cause group which pays attention to what is happening in Southern Africa, is knowledgeable about the system, is vigilant concerning official policy and its implementation, lobbies for further action and seeks to mobilise mass public opinion. The Irish Anti-Apartheid Movement (IAAM) has received considerable support across the political spectrum in Ireland; in all of the political parties there are deputies and senators who sponsor the movement, ask questions about Government policy and generally support an active policy on apartheid. The IAAM has established close links with the trade union movement; a liaison committee involving the Irish Congress of Trade Unions (ICTU) and the IAAM was set up in 1978. An industrial relations dispute (the Dunnes Stores' Strike) led to a wide-ranging discussion of Ireland's policy towards South Africa in 1985 and 1986. The trade union movement will continue to be important particularly if stringent sanctions against South Africa are at issue.

The 'attentive public' consists of two further related elements, the Churches and the development cooperation lobby. Both form part of the context within which Irish policy is made. There are over 800 Irish Missionaries working in South Africa and involved directly in the struggle against apartheid. The Irish Commission for Justice and Peace have made pronouncements on and is concerned with the moral and ethical dimension of Irish foreign policy. Cardinal O Fiaich, as President of the Roman Catholic Church's Hierarchy, has from time to time sent messages of support to the Catholic Hierarchy in South Africa[40] but most of the active work is carried out by Trocaire, the Catholic Agency for World Development. Trocaire is involved directly in South Africa in providing legal aid to the victims of apartheid and support for the black trade union movement. In 1986 Trocaire gave financial assistance to a seminar on post-apartheid South Africa.[41] South Africa is thus more sensitive than many other issues of global foreign policy which tend to be the prerogative of the executive and a small number of officials. It is conventional wisdom among academic observers that foreign policy in developing countries is made by a very small number of persons.[42] While formal competence for making foreign policy concerning South Africa is clearly the responsibility of the Cabinet, the Minister for Foreign Affairs and his officials, successive Irish Governments have been subjected to considerable domestic pressure on this issue.

This study will analyse the extent to which Ireland is prepared to go beyond declaratory diplomacy in its policy towards South Africa and assesses the range of policy options that have been used or may be used to influence events in South Africa. The study adopts two levels of analysis. First, Ireland's diplomacy in multilateral fora is assessed. Second, the domestic environment within which policy evolves is examined.

In Chapter Two Ireland's involvement at the UN on apartheid is analysed. In Chapter Three the regional context of Ireland's policy and the impact of European Political Cooperation (EPC) on Ireland's approach is examined. In Chapter Four the web of economic contact between Ireland and South Africa in addition to the implementation of UN and EC decisions is traced. Particular attention is paid to the adoption of a unilateral ban on the importation of South African fruit and vegetables. Chapter Five outlines the conclusions of the study and elaborates a series of policy recommendations.

■ CHAPTER 2 ■

Ireland's Stance on South Africa at the United Nations

W ith its near universal membership of 159 countries (1985), the United Nations provides one of the primary channels for debate in the international system. The participating states have the opportunity to make their voices heard on the major questions of world politics. The UN General Assembly has been characterised as the 'organised conscience of mankind'.[1] Each autumn the Foreign Ministers and diplomats of the member countries convene in an arena that affords them formal equality. The composition of the UN changed dramatically from the end of the 1950's onwards with the admission of the newly independent African and Asian states. These states became an important block in an organisation increasingly dominated by coalitions and block politics. Decolonisation and north-south issues assumed a central place on the UN agenda. The purpose of this chapter is to outline the role of the UN in the issue of apartheid and Ireland's policy at the UN. The first section gives a brief overview of UN policies on South Africa. The second section traces Ireland's approach to UN diplomacy in general and on apartheid resolutions in the General Assembly. The third section examines the voting pattern of a number of West European countries and the fourth section deals with the role of the Security Council.

The UN and South Africa

The UN provides a platform for a sustained political campaign against the racial policies of the South African regime, its unlawful presence in Namibia and its policy of destabilisation against neighbouring states. South Africa is a member of the United Nations; indeed some of its politicians and diplomats helped draft the UN Charter. But it has been gradually ostracised and isolated within the UN system, as the black African states became more outspoken on apartheid. Since September 1974 the credentials of South Africa's representatives have not been accepted by the General Assembly with the result that they cannot participate in its debates or committees. South Africa continues to maintain a mission in New York to enable its diplomats retain contact with the delegations from other countries.

The situation in South Africa has been discussed and scrutinised by all organs of the UN and its wider family of organizations including the International Court of Justice (Figure 1). The General Assembly passes a large number of resolutions calling for action against South Africa. The Assembly is confined to recommendations for the most part; its resolutions do not have the power of international law. Resolutions enable the General Assembly to set out the principles that should govern the behaviour of states. The Security Council in addition to passing resolutions has the power under the UN Charter to impose comprehensive or selective sanctions against any state. Article 41 of the Charter states that restrictive measures may include

> complete or partial interruption of economic relations and of rail, sea, air, postal, telegraphic, radio and other means of communication, and of severance of diplomatic relations.[2]

The distinction between the authoritative powers of the Security Council and the recommendations of the General Assembly has been stressed in answers to Dail Questions concerning sanctions against South Africa.[3] The UN Special Committee Against Apartheid, established by the General Assembly in 1962, engages in research on apartheid, assesses the implementation of General Assembly resolutions and actively campaigns against apartheid. The Council for Namibia was granted legal and political authority to administer the territory by the UN General Assembly until independence is achieved. The South African authorities have refused to allow the Council to take control of or even have access to the territory and they have prevaricated on the implementation of UN Security Council Resolution 435 issued in 1978 and agreed as a basis for the granting of independence.[4]

FIGURE 1
The main UN organs dealing with South Africa and Namibia

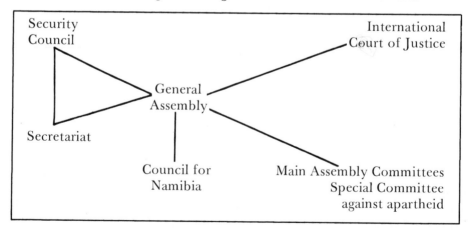

The General Assembly and the Security Council have passed a long line of condemnatory resolutions on South Africa over the last decades. UN opposition to apartheid existed practically since the system was adopted as official policy by the National Party in 1948. The General Assembly established the UN Commission on the Racial Situation in the Union of South Africa in 1952; this body has repeatedly taken the position that apartheid is a threat to continued peace in the Southern African region. With increasing African membership of the UN beginning in the 1960's, the tone of General Assembly resolutions became considerably stronger: in 1965, the Assembly expressed 'firm support' for opponents of apartheid; in 1970, it was calling for 'struggle by all means' to defeat apartheid and by 1976 'armed struggle'was endorsed.[5] Declarations and conventions on human rights, on the elimination of racial discrimination, and on the crime of apartheid gave tangible expression to these resolutions. A series of conferences under the auspices of the UN on apartheid have served to highlight the issue. Positive measures to aid the people suffering under apartheid include the UN Trust Fund for South Africa, the UN Educational and Training Programme for South Africa and the UN Fund for Publicity against Apartheid. The various funds channel finance and other forms of aid to the majority population in South Africa. Table 2 lists the main UN conventions dealing with human rights and the funds which channel monies to the victims of apartheid. (Ireland's contribution to the various UN Funds is dealt with in Appendix B.)

On the question of UN conventions dealing with human rights, Ireland does not have a good record. Several UN conventions have not been ratified

Table 2
UN Conventions and Funds relevant to the situation in South Africa

The UN Charter
Declaration on Human Rights (1948)
UN Declaration on the Elimination of all forms of Racial
    Discrimination (1963)
International Convention on Eliminating all forms of
    Discrimination (1965)
International Convention on the Suppression and Punishment of
    the Crime of Apartheid (1973)
UN Convention on Apartheid in Sport (1985)
UN Trust Fund for South Africa
UN Educational and Training Programme for South Africa
UN Trust Fund for Publicity against Apartheid
UN Fund for Namibia
UN Institute for Training and Research

including the Convention on the Elimination of all forms of Racial Discrimination passed in 1963. Mr. Peter Barry, then Minister for Foreign Affairs, in a reply to a Dail Question in July 1986, stated that Ireland intended to ratify the International Convention on Civil and Political Rights and the International Convention on the Elimination of all forms of Racial Discrimination. The former convention was being given priority, after which the Minister would examine the obstacles in domestic legislation to the ratification of the Convention on Racial Discrimination.[6] Delays in ratification have been explained by some writers as legislative inertia and reservations about specific provisions in the Conventions.[7]

Ireland and the United Nations

Ireland acceded to the UN in 1955 when agreement between the USA and the USSR opened the way for new members. Participation in UN politics afforded Ireland an opportunity to develop a distinctive role in world politics, to break out of post-war isolation, and to assume a place in the major international organisation of the post-war era. In 1956, the Minister for External Affairs, Mr. Liam Cosgrave, outlined the principles that would fashion Ireland's involvement in UN diplomacy. First, Ireland pledged support and respect for the Charter. Second, Ireland would maintain a position of independence judging each question on its merit. Third, Ireland's commitment to Western ideals and a Christian civilization was ennunciated.[8] The direction of Irish policy at the UN has tended to oscillate between independence of block politics and support for the position of the United States.[9]

Irish politicians and diplomats have shown particular interest in and attention to three areas of UN politics. First, from 1955 onwards Ireland associated itself with furthering the process of decolonisation. This led it to support the demands of the various colonies and to help them adapt to UN politics in the General Assembly once independence had been achieved. Ireland had used the Commonwealth and the League of Nations in the inter-war period to assert its own identity and independence.[10] An analysis of support for the demands of colonies or former colonies based on UN voting behaviour between 1948 and 1974 concluded that Ireland identified more frequently with the Third World block than the other EC states on this issue. Table 3 lists the anti-colonial index derived by Hurwitz for these countries.

Ireland's score (+ 0.67) is significantly higher than the original six EC member states and the UK. Denmark is the only EC country that approximates to Ireland's level. Namibia and South Africa are issues that fall within this tradition of Irish foreign policy. Second, Irish diplomats emphasize the importance of the UN Charter and peacekeeping; Ireland has contributed personnel to all major UN peacekeeping initiatives. Third,

Table 3
Level of Support for Self-determination (EC states)

Countries	Index
Original EC Countries	+ 0.13
UK.	− 0.20
Ireland.	+ 0.67
Denmark.	+ 0.49
Other UN	+ 0.70

Note: This study involved examining all roll-call votes between 1946 and 1974 at the UN General Assembly under the headings, decolonisation, self-determination, trusteeships, South Africa. The index is constructed as the difference between the number of YES votes and NO votes expressed as a proportion of the total number of votes.

Source: Hurwitz, Leon, 'The EEC and Decolonization', *Political Studies* 24 (No. 4, 1976, p.440)

as a non-member of a military alliance, Ireland has promoted disarmament and arms control.

UN Voting Because South Africa is one of the perennial issues on the UN agenda, Ireland together with the other member countries has to formulate a policy line each year when deciding how to vote on resolutions. Although these resolutions have no binding force, they are regarded as important statements of political intent. Once adopted, resolutions become a factor to which individual countries respond in making their foreign policies and a yardstick against which policy may be assessed by representative bodies and interest organisations in the domestic arena.

Resolutions on South Africa fall under three headings:—
1) Resolutions on Apartheid
2) Resolutions on Namibia
3) Resolutions on Decolonisation

The analysis of voting behaviour in this study examines all votes on the agenda item 'apartheid' between 1980 and 1986. There were a total of 80 resolutions on this issue in that time. The purpose of the analysis is to enable us to assess the principles which guide Ireland's voting pattern and to compare this pattern with that of a number of other states. Dail debates and questions are used to provide a historical dimension to the analysis.

In the General Assembly, a country may vote in favour of a resolution, against or abstain. In addition, a state may decide to be absent when a vote is called. Any one of these acts involves political choices.

A 'Yes' vote connotes agreement with the text of a resolution. A 'No' vote is generally accepted as strong demonstration of disagreement: Dr Garret FitzGerald said of a 'No' vote in the Dail in 1975 that 'if you vote against then it is so objectionable you cannot have any association with it'.[11] An abstention may mean mild doubt or a certain reservation concerning a resolution. It may also mean strong opposition to some particular parts of a resolution or it may be linked to the voting intentions of friendly states or coalition partners. No state votes in isolation; there may well be pressure from so-called 'likeminded' states. Individual countries have adopted a practice of declaring in the General Assembly the precise meaning of their votes. By analysing 'explanations of votes' (EOV's), it may be possible to analyse the reasoning behind particular positions.

The United Nations has evolved a policy style or characteristic way of doing things since its inception. There are formal rules of procedure which direct the work of the General Assembly. However, what happens in the Assembly is only the tip of the iceberg. Some resolutions on South Africa are discussed in the Special Political Committee before reaching a plenary session of the Assembly. The Afro-Asian block has considerable influence on the shape of resolutions; the Third World majority is sufficiently large to dominate the agenda of the General Assembly. In 1985 the General Assembly consisted of 51 African, 41 Asian, 33 Latin American, 11 East European and 23 OECD countries.

In addition to the formal work of the Assembly and its committees, informal discussion is an important feature of UN activity. According to one scholar, informal discussions

> make the formal business flow more quickly by providing a channel for reaching understandings about the procedures to be used at a particular moment or on a particular question, drafting more widely acceptable versions of a proposal or working out the tactics to be pursued in securing the passage of one's own or defeat of an opponent's proposal.[12]

The informal dimension of the preparation of resolutions has increased in importance owing to the development of block politics and regional groupings in General Assembly politics.

There is considerable discussion concerning the sponsorship of resolutions and the text within regional groupings. Ireland is a member of a number of overlapping groupings in the Assembly. First, Ireland belongs to the Western European and Other Groups (WEOG). This particular group is only active concerning the division of seats on various UN committees and bodies; it does not exercise a political role. Since 1973, Ireland has been a member of the European Community caucus as European Political Cooperation (EPC) has dealt with UN business from the outset. In addition, Ireland has informal contacts with a number of 'likeminded' states — largely the small neutral and NATO European countries. Ireland was invited to join the 'Likeminded Group' in 1976.

This group was an informal forum where the smaller European countries discussed North/South issues. Likeminded cooperation between small European states has a long history.[13] The impact of coalition politics on Ireland's voting pattern is dealt with in this and the next chapter of the study. Negotiations in the General Assembly are usually exercises in coalition building.

The management of UN activity Ireland maintains a permanent delegation in New York accredited to the UN and headed by a diplomat of ambassadorial rank. In Dublin, UN affairs are the responsibility of the Political Division of the Department of Foreign Affairs. This Division, which has 23 policy-making staff, is divided into four sections with responsibility for the major geographical regions of the world (Figure 2).

Figure 2
The Political Division — Department of Foreign Affairs (1986)

POLITICAL DIRECTOR (Assistant Secretary)			
Desk 1	*Desk 2*	*Desk 3*	*Desk 4*
EPC	Eastern Europe	Asia	Middle East
Western Europe	Conference on Security & Cooperation (CSCE)	Africa	UN
Americas			
Terrorism			

The UN section liaises with the Permanent Delegation in New York and co-ordinates the response to particular resolutions. Officials in the sections dealing with individual geographical areas have an important say concerning resolutions in their areas of responsibility. They would be regarded as the policy specialists. The management of UN business is not easy especially during meetings of the General Assembly when the agenda changes with speed. The delegation in New York acts as the eyes and ears of the home based officials by informing them of the views of other states, of requests to Ireland for support, for Ireland to act as a co-sponsor of resolutions and so on. There is a steady stream of advice on the policy line to adopt and on tactics to be pursued. The Ambassador devotes considerable time and energy to building up contacts with key officials in other delegations and in the UN Secretariat. The Irish delegation maintains contact with bodies like the Special Committee against Apartheid and could be involved in the preparatory work for international conferences on apartheid.

By and large, the Permanent Representation receives detailed instructions on voting intentions from the Department of Foreign Affairs. With modern systems of communication instructions may be sent with relative ease. The main policy lines are established in Dublin although the delegation in New York is allowed some room for manoeuvre especially in relation to procedural matters. Owing to the special place the UN occupies in Irish foreign policy, the Minister for Foreign Affairs usually plays an important role in shaping policy. On issues that are potentially sensitive in terms of political and public opinion, the Minister will always be consulted. Some Ministers have insisted on seeing detailed instructions. Because resolutions emerge over time, the Permanent Representation can inform the Minister of the likely shape of individual resolutions.

Garret FitzGerald, as Minister for Foreign Affairs, outlined the role of the Minister in reply to a Dail Question in 1975:

As the resolutions emerge or are likely to emerge I am consulted on the general line we will take. We try to anticipate the particular form resolutions will take and give general instructions on the line to follow in the debate and how to seek to amend them to meet our particular view. When the resolution comes forward in final form and a vote is sought, if time permits — normally it does, but very narrowly — I am consulted to give a decision.[14]

The control that is maintained over UN policy and voting intentions in the General Assembly indicates the importance accorded to UN diplomacy by Ireland.

Ireland's voting record There were 80 resolutions under the agenda item 'apartheid' between 1980 and 1986. The actual number of resolutions varies from year to year; there were 18 in 1980 and just 9 in 1986. A number of consistent themes surface in the resolutions, namely, condemnation of apartheid, sanctions, the arms embargo, relations between Israel and South Africa, apartheid in sport and various positive measures. A resolution may deal with one of these themes but frequently involves an amalgam of issues. Condemnation of the South African regime and those states that collaborate with it is usually matched by calls for action and positive measures in order to bring pressure to bear on South Africa.[15]

Writing in 1973, Keatinge concluded that in the United Nations, the Irish delegation while by no means in the vanguard of anti-apartheid activists, has been among the leading West European states in supporting resolutions condemning apartheid.[16] In 1979, Kadar Asmal, the Chairman of the Irish Anti-Apartheid Movement, expressed the fear that European Political Cooperation (EPC) would lead the smaller EC states to approximate their policies to those of the major powers on issues such as apartheid.[17] The analysis in this study should enable us to assess whether or not this fear was well founded. Table 4 sets out Ireland's voting pattern between 1980–1986.

Table 4
Ireland's voting pattern on 'apartheid' resolutions at the UN General Assembly 1980–1986

Year	Yes	(%)	No	(%)	Abstain	(%)	No Vote	(%)	Total
1980	7	(39)	1	(5)	7	(39)	3	(17)	18
1981	9	(56)	3	(19)	2	(13)	2	(13)	16
1982	5	(50)	1	(10)	3	(30)	1	(10)	10
1983	5	(45)	1	(9)	4	(36)	1	(9)	11
1984	5	(63)	2	(25)	0	—	1	(12)	8
1985	4	(44)	2	(22)	2	(22)	1	(12)	9
1986	3	(38)	2	(25)	2	(25)	1	(12)	8
TOTAL	38	(48)	12	(15)	20	(25)	10	(12)	80

Source: UN General Assembly Proceedings (1980–1986)

Ireland voted in favour of 48% of the resolutions, abstained on 25% and voted against 15%. If one excludes resolutions that were not voted on, Ireland voted in favour of 54%, abstained on 28% and against 17%. In order to explain this pattern of voting, it is necessary to assess the content of the resolutions themselves because much attention is paid to the language and vocabulary of each text.

Ireland votes in favour of resolutions that condemn the South African constitution, South African aggression against neighbouring states and the homelands policy. Ireland favours the work of the Special Committee against Apartheid, financial and other assistance to the victims of apartheid, public information about apartheid and the holding of international conferences to highlight the nature of the regime. Resolutions condemning sporting contacts with South Africa are viewed with favour. On calls for economic sanctions against Pretoria, Ireland favours an oil embargo, a ban on new investments and limited sanctions. Ireland votes against resolutions that call for comprehensive sanctions, that mention Israel and other states. Abstention is opted for on resolutions dealing with assistance to the liberation movement, military and nuclear collaboration with South Africa and calls on the mass media to highlight apartheid.

Ireland's total condemnation of apartheid is reiterated each year at the plenary session of the General Assembly and in each 'explanation of vote'. Ireland has in recent years co-sponsored a resolution on 'Concerted international action for the elimination of apartheid' (Appendix C). In addition to condemning the South African state, a series of demands are made which Ireland together with the other co-sponsors feel would open the way for change in South Africa. The demands are —

(a) The release of Nelson Mandela and other political prisoners
(b) A lifting of the state of emergency
(c) An abrogation of discriminatory laws, and an end to restrictions on the censorship of news media
(d) Freedom of association and full trade union rights
(e) The introduction, without pre-conditions, of a political dialogue with genuine leaders of the majority population
(f) The eradication of bantustan structures
(g) An immediate withdrawal of troops from Southern Angola and an end to the destabilisation of the frontline and other states.[18]

These demands are used to judge the behaviour of the South African Government and political developments within South Africa.

Each year the question of punitive sanctions against South Africa is raised in a number of different resolutions. On the issue of sanctions, Ireland believes that

> the right policy for the international community is one of steady and graduated pressure for change through carefully chosen, selective, graduated sanctions; such sanctions to be mandatory, ie. properly imposed by the Security Council and fully implemented by all.[19]

In answers to Dail questions and in the 'explanations of vote' the importance attached to mandatory sanctions is underlined again and again.

Ireland has supported resolutions on a mandatory oil embargo and in 1980 co-sponsored a resolution which called for a ban on new investments in and loans to South Africa.[20] Resolutions calling for a strengthening of the arms embargo have also been supported although Ireland abstained on the original resolution in 1976 calling on the Security Council to establish a mandatory arms embargo. This was justified in the Dail by the Minister for Foreign Affairs on the grounds that certain countries had been mentioned in the resolution. One of the countries concerned, the Federal Republic of Germany denied that it had collaborated with South Africa. In reply to a Dail Question, Dr FitzGerald pointed out that:

> For the first time this year's resolution contained references to particular countries as exporting arms to South Africa. In one instance, in particular, the government in question, a friendly country, made representations to us saying that it was false. That government's statement has been circulated by the anti-apartheid committee of the United Nations in New York without comment. This would seem to suggest acceptance of the fact that the allegation made in the preamble to the resolution against that country was not correct. When such a false allegation is made against a friendly country, while we support the general tenor of the resolution, it would be inappropriate for us to

vote for it and we marked our disapprobation of what appeared to be an incorrect allegation by abstaining.[21]

In this case abstention was used to express disapproval of a particular section of a resolution while supporting the resolution in other respects.

The resolution on 'Concerted international action against apartheid' contains a series of punitive measures against South Africa and positive measures in favour of those people affected by apartheid. As Ireland co-sponsors the resolution, it provides the most accurate statement of Ireland's policy vis-a-vis economic instruments. The resolution calls on the UN states to consider national legislative and other measures to increase pressure on the apartheid regime, such as

(a) Cessation of further investment in, or financial loans to South Africa
(b) An end to all promotion of and support for trade with South Africa
(c) Prohibition of the sale of Krugerrands and all other coins minted in South Africa
(d) Cessation of all forms of military, police or intelligence cooperation with the authorities of South Africa, in particular the sale of computer equipment
(e) An end to nuclear collaboration with South Africa
(f) Cessation of export and sale of oil to South Africa.

This resolution[22] commands wide support in the General Assembly; it was adopted by 149 votes with two negative votes (USA and UK) and five abstentions (Cote d'Ivoire, Federal Republic of Germany, Israel, Lesotho and Malawi). The resolution is supported by all of the EC states with the exception of Germany and the UK. Two of the frontline states (Lesotho and Malawi) feel unable to support the resolution.[23]

Ireland's preference for limited measures is seen in the above resolution and in resolutions calling for mandatory and comprehensive sanctions. Ireland either abstains or votes against these resolutions. In 1980, Ireland abstained on a resolution calling for comprehensive sanctions which asked the European Community to take the necessary steps to deny all assistance and commercial and other facilities to the racist regime of South Africa.[24] Ireland voted against this resolution in 1981 and expressed

doubts about the wisdom of calls for comprehensive sanctions at the present juncture. Had the draft resolution on comprehensive and mandatory sanctions corresponded to the resolution adopted at the last session of the Assembly, my delegation would have abstained. However, a new and divisive element had been introduced to the draft resolution this year, that is, the arbitrary condemnation of a number of countries. . . . Because of this my delegation has decided to vote against the draft resolution.[25]

The United States, the United Kingdom and the Federal Republic of Germany are mentioned in the resolution for the first time.[26] In 1982

39

and 1983 Ireland reverted to an abstentionist position because individual states are not mentioned.[27]

From 1984 to 1986, Ireland voted against this resolution. The reason given was that Ireland did not favour the complete isolation of South Africa because it would have the effect of 'abandoning black South Africans to the whim of the South African authorities'.[28] Ireland's position on comprehensive sanctions hardened somewhat in this period.

In 1987 Ireland reverted to a policy of abstention because the tone of the resolution changed. Apparently, the African states made an attempt to increase the level of agreement on the agenda item by toning down the language used. In particular, Resolution L28 on 'comprehensive sanctions' did not condemn individual countries for collaboration with South Africa. Ireland's Permanent Representative to the UN said in the General Assembly that 'the resolution contains fewer objectionable elements than the corresponding text which the UN adopted last year'.[29] Although reverting to abstention, Ireland does not favour comprehensive sanctions at this juncture.

Ireland consistently votes against resolutions that mention particular states. Each year there is a resolution on 'Relations between Israel and South Africa' against which Ireland registers strong disapproval because the 'text singles out one Member State of this Assembly for selective condemnation in an inappropriate manner'.[30] Ireland has voted against resolutions on 'Military and Nuclear Collaboration with South Africa' for the same reason. In 1981 a resolution with this title refers to the 'collusion by the Governments of certain Western countries and other states, particularly those of the United States of America, the Federal Republic of Germany and Israel'[31] with South Africa. More recently, Ireland abstained on a resolution with this title but continues to object to the 'unfair, selective and arbitrary singling out and criticism of a number of states'.[32]

Each year there is a complex resolution on the 'Situation in South Africa' which refers to political developments. Ireland has tended to abstain on this resolution for a number of reasons. The resolution contains references to the armed struggle; the 1986 resolution 'reaffirms the legitimacy of their struggle against the apartheid regime as well as their right to choose the necessary means, including armed struggle to attain their noble objectives'.[33] Ireland's representatives have consistently claimed that they cannot endorse the armed struggle. In 1986 the EOV states

> My delegation has made it clear in the past that we do not wish to see the Assembly endorse violence. Even if we can understand the sense of growing hopelessness and bitter frustration from which such violence might spring, my Government cannot condone it.[34]

This resolution frequently calls for comprehensive sanctions and usually names certain states to which Ireland also objects. By abstaining, Ireland demonstrates its agreement with much of the text but its objections to certain clauses.

Apartheid in sport has been the subject of a long line of resolutions in the General Assembly. Ireland has either voted in favour or abstained on these resolutions. Ireland supported the establishment of an ad hoc committee to draw up a convention on apartheid in sport. When the convention was presented to the General Assembly in 1985, Ireland was unable to support it because of the terms of the text. While supporting the principle of non-discrimination in sport, Articles 3, 6 and 10 proved to be incompatible with the Irish constitution.[35] The articles require the Government to prohibit sporting contacts, a power which an Irish Government does not have (Appendix D gives the text of the three articles). In an earlier EOV, the Irish delegation stated that Ireland could not restrict the constitutional right of Irish citizens to freely travel abroad.[36] Legal objection to the text of the resolution and the convention explain Ireland's change in voting behaviour.

Ireland has voted in favour of an academic, cultural and sports boycott of South Africa.[37] Ireland abstained on a 1981 resolution on the mass media because it was felt that this would interfere with the freedom of the press.[38] The more recent resolution on 'Concerted international action against apartheid' appeals to all Governments and organisations to take appropriate action for the cessation of all academic, cultural, scientific and sports relations that would support the apartheid regime of South Africa, as well as relations with individuals, institutions and other bodies endorsing or based on apartheid.[39]

Ireland supports the work of the UN Special Committee Against Apartheid; it votes in favour of the yearly resolution on its work while stating that Ireland's attitude 'to the recommendations in the report of the Special Committee must be understood in accordance with the policy of the Government on apartheid'.[40] Thus support for the Committee does not imply agreement with all of its work or recommendations. Ireland is not a member of the Committee which is dominated by the Third World block. Representatives of the Special Committee visited Ireland in 1974 which was regarded as recognition of Ireland's stance on apartheid and of the work of the Irish Anti-Apartheid Movement.[41]

Positive measures to aid people who are the victims of apartheid are a feature of UN activity. Each year there are a number of resolutions on various funds; these resolutions tend to be passed by consensus or by overwhelming majorities. Ireland traditionally co-sponsors the resolution on the Trust Fund for South Africa. A small proportion of Ireland's multilateral aid is channeled to these Funds (Appendix B gives details of the amounts that were allocated between 1980 and 1985). Ireland favours humanitarian aid but will not 'support guerrilla activities in Southern Africa'.[42]

Ireland tends to place considerable emphasis on strict rules of procedure and respect for the Charter, one of the principles elaborated in

1956. Irish policy makers do not condone the use of procedural devices to exclude South Africa. The official view is that each state is entitled to participate in the proceedings of the Assembly until their membership rights are suspended in accordance with the explicit provisions of Articles Five and Six of the UN Charter. Nor does Ireland favour the expulsion of South Africa from the UN. The principle of universality of membership is important in Irish policy. Moreover, it is felt that South Africa should be exposed to the pressure of world opinion.[43] In 1982, Ireland abstained on a UN resolution requesting the IMF to refrain from granting credits to South Africa. In reply to a Dail Question, Ireland's position was justified as being 'procedural' and designed to safeguard the independent competence of the IMF.[44] Ireland did not support the South African application itself.

UN Voting: a Comparative Perspective

The resolutions on apartheid are adopted either unanimously or by overwhelming majorities in the General Assembly. The African states are virtually united in their opposition to the South African regime and they receive the backing of the Third World coalition and the Soviet block. Opposition to, or abstention on, the resolutions comes largely from the OECD states; countries that have the capacity because of their economic ties with South Africa to implement the resolutions.

For the purposes of the study, the voting behaviour of all of the European Community states, together with the three neutrals (Austria, Sweden, Finland) and Norway was recorded. Switzerland is not a member of the UN. In order to assess the extent to which these countries supported UN General Assembly resolutions, an index was calculated for each country using the method adopted by Hurwitz in his work on the European Community and decolonisation.[45] The level of each country's support for apartheid resolutions was calculated by assigning a value of + 1.0 to each 'yes' vote, a value of − 1.0 for each negative vote and a value of 0 to a recorded abstention. The sum of these values was then expressed as a proportion of the total number of votes. This is a crude index designed to indicate in general terms where each country lies in relation to other countries on this issue. It also enables us to identify possible groupings. In addition to the index, the percentage of 'yes' votes, 'no' votes and abstentions are recorded for each country. Table 5 sets out the number of votes cast by the West European states and their voting behaviour.

The voting pattern of the West European states is extremely varied on the issue of apartheid. Ireland stands at 0.37 which is the fifth highest of the 16 countries recorded in the table. Greece and Spain with a score of 0.50 are the highest with Sweden and Finland standing at 0.47. The most striking feature of this table is the difference between the four largest

Table 5

The voting pattern on 'apartheid' resolutions at the UN General Assembly 1980–1986, selected countries (70 Roll Calls)

Countries	Yes	%	No	%	Abstain	%	Index
EC							
Belgium	20	(28.6)	32	(45.7)	18	(25.7)	− 0.17
France	14	(20.0)	35	(50.0)	21	(30.0)	− 0.30
Germany	6	(33.0)	33	(47.1)	31	(44.3)	− 0.38
Italy	19	(27.1)	22	(31.4)	29	(41.4)	− 0.04
Luxembourg	19	(27.1)	31	(44.3)	20	(28.6)	− 0.17
Netherlands	29	(41.4)	21	(30.0)	20	(28.6)	0.11
Denmark	34	(48.6)	13	(18.6)	23	(32.9)	0.30
Ireland	38	(54.3)	12	(17.1)	20	(28.6)	0.37
UK	0	(00.0)	47	(67.1)	23	(32.9)	− 0.67
Greece	38	(54.3)	3	(4.3)	29	(41.4)	0.50
Spain	40	(57.1)	5	(7.1)	25	(35.7)	0.50
Portugal	22	(33.4)	22	(31.4)	26	(37.1)	0.00
Others							
Sweden	40	(57.1)	7	(10.0)	23	(32.9)	0.47
Austria	31	(44.3)	7	(10.0)	32	(45.7)	0.34
Finland	40	(57.1)	7	(10.0)	23	(32.9)	0.47
Norway	38	(54.3)	14	(20.0)	18	(25.7)	0.34

Source: Calculated from UN voting results contained in the UN publication *Proceedings of the General Assembly (1980–86)*

Note to Table 5

The ranking of countries is partly a function of the way the index is constructed. Any index requires a subjective decision on the relative values to be given to 'yes' and 'no' votes and abstentions. For example an index might be based on the proportion of 'yes' votes in the total and this would give a different ranking of countries (see first percentages columns in Table 5). The index used in the text is preferred because it recognises that countries which abstain and those which vote no are taking different positions. The inevitably subjective nature of any index should be borne in mind in interpreting the figures in Table 5.

EC countries (United Kingdom, the Federal Republic of Germany, France and Italy) and most of the smaller states in Western Europe. Only Belgium and Luxembourg, of the other smaller states, record a negative index. The four largest countries have a combined index of − 0.34; the UK, France and Germany record many more negative votes than Italy which frequently opts for abstention. Furthermore, France changed its position somewhat after 1983; between 1984 and 1986 the French delegation recorded far fewer 'no' votes. The position of the UK and Germany does not soften. During the entire period under review, the United Kingdom fails to record a single positive vote.

The smaller states vary one from the other. Belgium and Luxembourg with an identical index of − 0.17 use the larger states as a reference point. The Irish index of 0.37 is closer to that of the neutral states (0.41) than it is to the smaller EC states (0.18). If one excludes Belgium and Luxembourg, however, the index for the smaller EC states rises to 0.30. By examining the percentages for each country in Table 5 it is possible to assess how each country uses the different voting options. A group of countries including Sweden, Finland, Norway, Denmark, Spain, Greece, the Netherlands and Ireland vote in favour of apartheid resolutions most frequently. Abstention is used most frequently by Italy, Austria and Portugal while strong disapproval is registered by the United Kingdom, Germany, France, Belgium and Luxembourg by opting for a predominance of negative votes. Table 6 abstracts this data from Table 5.

Table 6

Use of 'yes' votes, 'no' votes and abstention by the West European countries on apartheid resolutions

'Yes	%	'No'	%	Abstention	%
Sweden	57.1	UK	67.1	Austria	45.7
Finland	57.1	France	50.1	Germany	44.3
Spain	57.1	Germany	47.1	Italy	41.4
Greece	56.3	Belgium	45.7	Greece	41.4
Ireland	56.3	Luxembourg	44.3	Portugal	37.1
Norway	56.3	Portugal	31.4	Spain	35.7
Denmark	48.6	Italy	31.4	UK	32.9
Austria	44.3	Netherlands	30.1	Denmark	32.9
Netherlands	41.4	Norway	20.1	Sweden	32.9
Portugal	31.4	Denmark	18.6	Finland	32.9
Belgium	28.6	Ireland	17.1	France	30.1
Italy	27.1	Sweden	10.1	Ireland	28.6
Luxembourg	27.1	Austria	10.1	Netherlands	28.6
France	20.1	Finland	10.1	Luxembourg	28.6
Germany	8.6	Spain	7.1	Norway	25.7
UK	—	Greece	4.3	Belgium	25.7

Source: Calculated from UN voting results contained in the UN publication Proceedings of the General Assembly (1980–1986)

Voting behaviour must be analysed in relation to substantive issues of policy. In 1986 none of the sixteen states in Table 5 voted in favour of comprehensive and mandatory sanctions. All of the EC states with the exception of Greece voted against the resolution which indicates strong disapproval for this line of action. The three neutral states (Sweden, Finland and Austria) abstained and Norway voted against. Equally none of these countries voted in favour of the resolution on the situation in South Africa and assistance to the liberation movements. The large EC states together with Belgium and Luxembourg voted against. The remaining EC states and the neutrals abstained. All of the states voted against the resolution condemning Israel, with the exception of Greece which abstained. The resolution on the convention on sport and apartheid evoked abstentions from all of the states for constitutional reasons. The question of an oil embargo was opposed by France, Germany and the UK. Austria, Finland, Sweden, Denmark, Ireland and Norway voted in favour and the remaining EC countries abstained.

The resolution on 'Concerted international action' is sponsored by a number of the smaller European states and others. Among the Community states, Ireland, Greece, and Denmark sponsor the resolution. The three neutrals, Sweden, Austria and Finland give their support. Norway and Iceland are the remaining European states sponsoring the resolution. Australia and New Zealand provide additional support from the industrial states. Tanzania, Zambia, Nigeria, Zimbabwe, Gambia, Madagascar and Ghana provide the African support for the resolution. Egypt and Malaysia also support the resolution. This is clearly a bridge-building exercise between a number of small industrialised states and the so-called Third World coalition. This resolution has tended to get the support of the EC states with the exception of the UK which votes against and Germany which opts for abstention.[46] The impact of EPC activity on voting behaviour at the UN is dealt with in Chapter Three.

The Security Council

The Security Council has five permanent members and ten members elected for short periods. Britain and France are members of the European Community and of the Security Council. Ireland served on the Security Council for a half-term in the early 1960's and again in 1981/1982. The Security Council is the only UN body with the power under the Charter to impose sanctions against any state that is perceived as a threat to world peace. Many General Assembly resolutions are addressed to the Security Council with requests for action. Ireland has always maintained that Security Council decisions that are binding on all states are necessary for effective international measures. In reply to a Dail

Question in 1978, David Andrews, as Minister of State in the Department of Foreign Affairs, argued that

> Successive Irish Governments have always held that for international measures to be effective they must be mandatory and therefore imposed by the UN Security Council or otherwise they will achieve little and may even lead to widescale evasion.[47]

This is the approach adopted by most industrial countries.

The Security Council has passed many resolutions on South Africa but has failed except on one occasion to impose binding action. In 1963 a resolution was agreed concerning a voluntary arms embargo against South Africa. After repeated General Assembly resolutions calling on the Security Council to make the embargo mandatory, resolution 418 was adopted unanimously in 1977 imposing such an embargo. The text of the resolution declared that the acquisition by South Africa of arms and related material constituted a threat to the maintenance of international peace and security.[48] The embargo has numerous loopholes which have impaired its effectiveness. It was followed by Security Council resolution 558 (1984) requesting all of the member states to refrain from importing arms, ammunition of all types and military vehicles produced in South Africa.[49] The question of further sanctions is raised from time to time. In July 1985 France, in response to the declaration of the state of emergency in South Africa, tabled a resolution at the Security Council calling for specific measures against South Africa. The resolution endorsing limited and voluntary sanctions (569) was passed because the United Kingdom and the USA abstained.

The resolution urged all UN states to:
(1) Suspend new investments and export loan guarantees;
(2) Prohibit the sale of RSA gold coins;
(3) Restrict cultural and sporting contacts;
(4) Prohibit new contacts in the nuclear field;
(5) Prohibit the sale of computer equipment that may be used by the army and police.[50]

The US and the UK used the veto later in 1985 to defeat a resolution on mandatory sanctions. It is unlikely in the foreseeable future that comprehensive and mandatory sanctions will be approved by the Council given the US and UK vetoes.

Conclusions

The UN is undoubtedly the main platform in the international system for a sustained political and moral campaign against the policies and practices of the South African Government. It is the most appropriate arena for global and mandatory sanctions against the regime if a consensus is arrived at on the use of effective economic action. The Security Council has the power to impose binding obligations on the UN Member States but certainly not the will given the veto power of the USA and the UK. Despite a long line of condemnatory resolutions against apartheid by all of the UN bodies over many decades, the South African authorities have been relatively immune and have shown little willingness to change the essential characteristics of 'separate development'.

Ireland has used the UN to make known its policies on South Africa. The analysis of voting behaviour in this study suggests that there is considerable consistency in the pattern of voting between 1980 and 1986. Moreover, the principles which guide Ireland's response to particular resolutions are part of a well established policy line on apartheid and on the UN itself. Respect for the Charter and the need for procedural correctness amount to a guiding principle of policy. The singling out of individual states for condemnation in resolutions is strongly objected to by Ireland. This theme is so prevalent in EOV's that it constitutes a principle which guides voting behaviour. The universality of international organisations is another oft-stated principle. A refusal to condone the use of force is also evident in voting behaviour.

On substantive issues of policy, the major change observed in the period under review is the use of a 'no' vote rather than abstention on the question of comprehensive sanctions between 1984 and 1986. Ireland supports the use of economic policy instruments to bring pressure to bear on South Africa but such measures should be selective and graduated. The resolution on 'Concerted international action to eliminate apartheid' provides a useful summary of the measures Ireland is willing to take. A second policy change on the resolution dealing with apartheid in sport may be explained by the legal implications of the UN Convention.

Ireland favours the majority of resolutions on apartheid. In fact Ireland's preferred policy is to vote in favour of these resolutions. Abstention is used to register disapproval of resolutions which contain much that Ireland feels unable to endorse. Negative votes which connote strong disapproval of a resolution are cast sparingly. From the examination of Dail debates and questions, it is possible to detect a certain unease with some resolutions. Dr Garret FitzGerald, when Minister for Foreign Affairs, spoke of the 'confrontatory tactics' of a number of countries; he maintained that Ireland was being 'forced into a position of not supporting resolutions which in a different form Ireland had traditionally favoured'.[51]

■ CHAPTER 3 ■
The European Community, Ireland and South Africa

E conomic, political and cultural bonds tie the Republic of South Africa to many states in Western Europe. Britain the former colonial power, continues to have considerable interaction with South Africa. Germany, Portugal and Belgium had colonial ties with neighbouring states. The Netherlands was the original home of the Afrikaner. France, although not directly involved in Southern Africa, continues to exert extensive influence in Africa. All of these countries have distinctive bilateral ties with South Africa. Relations with this part of the African continent are also moulded by the existence of the European Community. The foreign trade relations of EC states are now governed by the common commercial policy based on Article 113 of the Rome Treaty. Development cooperation policies are influenced by the Lome Convention which establishes a multilateral framework for relations with a large number of African states including the so-called frontline countries. European Political Cooperation (EPC) has become a central element in the foreign policies of all of the EC Member States. Thus, while each state retains considerable freedom of action in the international system, the European Community has become a major actor in its own right.

The purpose of this chapter is to assess EC policies towards South Africa. The first section is devoted to a brief assessment of the web of economic contacts between South Africa and EC countries. The second section analyses the development of policy within the framework of European Political Cooperation (EPC) and the approach of the European Parliament. The third section analyses the regional context. The fourth section provides a brief overview of the policies of other states and the final section gives an outline of Ireland's influence on the evolution of EC policy.

Economic Dimension Material considerations loom large in the minds of European policy makers when assessing various policy options. Economic contact with South Africa is usually viewed in one of two ways. On the one hand, it is argued that trade with and investment in South Africa supported the growth of the apartheid economy by initiating the process of capital formation, by transferring technology and managerial skills and by providing the basis for trade. In addition, by maintaining a presence in South Africa, multinational companies are a key factor in sustaining business confidence.[1] On the other hand, it is argued that economic links provide a means for exerting pressure on the South African system. By developing the skills of the black population, investment can act as an agent of change. This is the main argument used in favour of Codes of Conduct for foreign companies operating in South Africa. These two views surface again and again in the debate on policy options vis-a-vis the apartheid regime.

South Africa has extensive economic links with the European Community. In 1984, just eight countries, including five EC states, Britain, Germany, France, Italy, Belgium, the United States, Switzerland and Japan took 71 percent of South Africa's non-gold exports and supplied 78 percent of its imports. The EC countries on their own took over 40 percent of exports and imports making the EC South Africa's largest trading partner.[2] In contrast just 1.5 percent of EC imports originate in South Africa and 2.3 percent of total exports are sold to South Africa. The importance of trading links varies from one EC country to another.

Table 7 sets out the value of imports from South Africa in 1985 and 1986. Italy (24.3%) and Belgium and Luxembourg (27.9%) account for

Table 7
Imports from South Africa EC (12)
(in 1,000 ECUs)

Country	1985 Value	% of EC Total	1986 Value	% of EC Total
Belgium/ Luxembourg	2,225,778	23.5	2,235,065	27.9
Denmark	206,789	2.2	102,169	1.3
Germany	1,359,033	14.4	1,288,783	16.1
Greece	56,785	0.6	54,486	0.7
Spain	248,307*	2.6	262,098	3.3
France	825,614	8.7	479,746	6.0
Ireland	18,201	0.2	14,060	0.2
Italy	2,424,264	25.6	1,951,223	24.3
Netherlands	237,620	2.5	219,981	2.7
Portugal	61,967*	0.7	61,486	0.8
UK	1,791,897	19.0	1,252,735	16.7
TOTAL	9,456,255	100.0	8,021,832	100.0

Source: Eurostat, *Nimexe External Trade, 2 Vols, 1985 and 1986*
*Figures for Spain and Portugal were supplied by DGI, EC Commission.

the largest shares followed by the UK (16.7%) and Germany (16.1%). Official figures underestimate British imports from South Africa because that country does not supply country of origin for the importation of diamonds. In 1986 the value of UK imports of diamonds listed in Eurostat under the heading of 'secret' was 2,284,000 ecu's. If a high proportion of these imports originated in South Africa the percentage breakdown in Table 7 would alter. The value of imports from South Africa fell by 15 percent between 1985 and 1986 and according to the EC Commission continued to fall in 1987.[3] South African trade statistics no longer include information on the ranking of South Africa's trading partners since the imposition of economic sanctions.

The main exporters to South Africa are the Federal Republic of Germany (42.1% of total trade in 1986) and the UK (26.5%). The other two large EC countries are much less significant (16.4%) (See Table 8). The remaining 14 percent of exports is made up of the smaller EC states. Ireland contributes less than one percent of Community exports to South Africa. The value of exports fell by 18 percent between 1985 and 1986.

A commodity breakdown of South African trade displays the tra-

Table 8
Exports to South Africa EC (12)
(in 1,000 ECUs)

Country	1985 Value	% of EC Total	1986 Value	% of EC Total
Belgium/ Luxembourg	243,499	4.3	218,107	4.7
Denmark	77,328	1.4	53,429	1.1
Germany	2,246,069	39.5	1,970,369	42.1
Greece	2,257	0.04	2,456	0.1
Spain	124,000*	2.2	87,324	1.9
France	510,064	9.0	411,031	8.8
Ireland	41,303	0.7	41,136	0.9
Italy	434,110	7.6	357,401	7.6
Netherlands	279,074	4.9	260,147	5.6
Portugal	20,000*	0.4	15,866	0.3
UK	1,709,218	30.0	1,257,481	26.9
TOTAL	5,687,822	100.0	4,674,747	100.0

Source: Eurostat, Nimexe External Trade, 2 Vols, 1985 and 1986
*Figures for Spain and Portugal (1985) were supplied by EC Commission.

ditional pattern of North/South commerce. EC exports comprise machinery and computers, motor vehicles, electrical equipment and plastics (Appendix E gives a commodity breakdown by principal exporter to South Africa). An analysis of South Africa's exports to the EC reveals a heavy concentration on raw and processed minerals in addition to fruit and vegetables. The UK and Germany are the major importers of fruit and vegetables. Italy, France and Germany account for a sizeable proportion of mineral imports — ferro-alloys, chemical products and copper. The UK imports over half of all metallic ore. Belgium and Luxembourg account for almost all chemicals and over a quarter of total imports of copper. (Appendix F lists EC imports from South Africa and the principal importers.)

South Africa produces a wide range of minerals; it is the world's primary or second most important producer of platinum, manganese, chrome, vanadium and gold. (Appendix G provides a breakdown of South Africa's production of these minerals.) Platinum is an important element for many industries (petro-chemicals, car exhaust convertors, electronic and laboratory equipment). Manganese, vanadium and chromium are used in the steel industry. Although South Africa is a major producer of these minerals, there are other sources of supply notably the Soviet Union. Platinum poses special problems because South Africa is a major exporter and has over 85 percent of global reserves. A cut off of supplies would cause shortages and world prices would rocket.[4] Moorsom (1986) concludes that a trade embargo which included platinum would cause awkward short term problems for the car industry and a few other specialised industries. Hanlon and Omond (1987) suggest that a platinum ban should be a last step.[5] There is considerable disagreement in the literature concerning the issue of strategic minerals. Figures vary on South Africa's reserves of these minerals and on the Community's dependence on this source of supply.[6] Hanlon and Omond (1986) and Moorsom (1986) conclude that a minerals cut off could be managed by the industrial countries and that industry would not grind to a halt.[7] In contrast Maull (1986) claims that strategic minerals are the West's Achilles Heel.[8]

South Africa has attracted extensive investment from overseas; it is estimated that over 2,000 foreign companies have subsidiary branches or are associated with South African companies. Foreign investment (direct and indirect) totalled $40 billion in 1985. Of this $15 billion originated in the UK, $13 billion in the USA, $2.5 billion in Germany and $2 billion in France. Approximately 70 percent of total investment in South Africa is either American or British. External loan finance has become an even more important part of foreign liabilities. In 1970 foreign loans amounted to 40 percent of the total stock of South African foreign liabilities; the proportion rose to 70 percent by 1984.[9] Demand for external capital comes from the Government and large state companies (parastatals) to finance expansion programmes and to fund trade deficits. Between 1980 and 1984 short term borrowing rose from $6 billion to over $13 billion.

By September 1986, South Africa had a foreign debt in the region of $24 billion.[10]

Economic ties with the European Community and other industrial countries are essential to South Africa. The EC is its largest trading partner with the UK and Germany as the major exporters. These two countries together with Italy and Belgium are the major importers of South African goods. Britain followed by the USA is the major source of foreign investment. Apart from a number of minerals, notably the platinum group, South Africa is not that important to the economies of the West European States. It is not a major market for EC products.

The Political Dimension: From Complacency to Action

Political Cooperation among the Member States of the Community dates from the Hague Summit of 1969 when the Heads of Government requested their Foreign Ministers to examine the best way of achieving progress in the matter of political unification.[11] The Luxembourg Report (1970) advocated the development of a form of cooperation in foreign affairs. European Political Cooperation (EPC) is the process whereby the Member States inform each other of their views on the major issues of international politics and try to arrive at a common position. From time to time the Member States have combined to use economic policy instruments.

The Single European Act formalises and institutionalises the conventions and practices of European Political Cooperation by providing it with a Treaty basis. Title III of the Act explicitly states that the High

EPC Machinery

> The machinery of EPC has evolved in a pragmatic and piecemeal fashion since 1970. The Presidency has a pivotal role in the process; the country holding the chair has responsibility for arranging and chairing all meetings of EPC and of representing the Community in international fora. The Foreign Ministers of the Member States meet approximately four times each year and their senior diplomats (Political Directors) meet approximately eight times in the Political Committee. A European Correspondents Group is responsible under the direction of the Political Committee for monitoring the implementation of EPC. There are a large number of working groups dealing with various issues on the agenda. A telex system (COREUR) links the Foreign Ministries of the Member States. A small EPC secretariat has been established in Brussels.

Contracting Parties shall endeavour jointly to formulate and implement a European foreign policy. This is probably highly aspirational as such a policy would require a high degree of homogeneity of interests among the various actors. The Act states that the Member States 'shall ensure that common principles are gradually developed and defined' and that they shall 'increase their capacity for joint action in the foreign policy field'. There is, however, no compulsion on the Member States to agree; the Treaty binds them to 'endeavour', 'to take full account of', or 'to avoid any action' and so on. Consensus is one of the well established 'rules of the game' among the Member States. The Act provides for the establishment of a small EPC Secretariat in Brussels.

Title III of the Single European Act was the subject of a referendum in Ireland and engendered a wide-ranging assessment and public debate on the impact of EPC on Irish foreign policy. By a majority of 3 to 2, the Supreme Court found that ratification of Title III would be unconstitutional unless the Constitution was suitably amended.[12] The judgements of the Court offered two very different interpretations of the nature of Title III and EPC. The majority decision (Henchy, Walsh and Hederman JJJ.) found that institutionalising EPC in a formal Treaty framework involved a transformation of the nature of the European Community from essentially an economic union to a political one. Henchy concluded that

> A perusal of Title III of the SEA satisfies me that each ratifying member state will be bound to surrender part of its sovereignty in the conduct of foreign relations.[13]

But Justices Finlay and Griffin (minority decision) found that the terms of Title III did not oblige the state to cede sovereignty in the sphere of foreign affairs. Justice Finlay argued that

> It appears probable that under modern conditions a State seeking co-operation with other States in the sphere of foreign policy must be prepared to enter not merely vague promises but actual arrangements for consultation and discussion.[14]

During the referendum campaign most attention was devoted to the impact of the SEA on Ireland's non-involvement in military alliances. There was in addition consideration of the impact of EPC on Irish foreign policy since accession to the EC in 1973. It was argued by opponents of the constitutional amendment that EPC had weakened Ireland's 'independent' or 'traditional' foreign policy with regard to such issues as Southern Africa.

Political Cooperation brings together twelve countries with different traditions in foreign policy and varying historical experiences. Factors such as size, geographical location and level of economic development condition the responses of the participants to events in the wider world. The Member States actively pursue their interests within the framework of EPC. MacKernan (1984) has aptly pointed out that it is the degree of homogeneity between the national interests of the individual member states, actual or potential, existing or susceptible of being deliberately fostered and created, that will determine their willingness to broaden the scope of political cooperation, to strengthen their commitment to the process, and to increase the range of instruments at its disposal.[15]

EPC procedures are essentially intergovernmental and have been jealously guarded by the national Foreign Ministries. Political Cooperation is a slow, painstaking and frequently tortuous process because of the need for consensus. However, arising from the steady build-up of trust among the Member States, there is a strong commitment to consult and to exchange information among the participants. Because of the continual and intensive exchange of views involved in EPC, informal group pressures which foster agreement exist.

EPC is essentially a reactive rather than an anticipatory process. Consequently, events in South Africa itself have tended to direct the agenda in the Community. In February 1976, the first joint declaration on Southern Africa was issued by the Member States. The declaration dealt mostly with Angola but emphasised the willingness of the Community to cooperate with the countries of the region. The text stressed the right to self-determination and independence of the people of Rhodesia and Namibia and included the first EC condemnation of apartheid.[16] Since then there has been a steady stream of declarations, joint statements and demarches emanating from the European Council and the Conference of Foreign Ministers. The EPC working party on Africa has been dominated by events in Southern Africa.

What is being said? There has been no shortage of declarations condemning apartheid since 1976. Gaston Thorn, addressing the UN in 1980 on behalf of the Nine stressed that

> The policy of apartheid pursued in South Africa is a matter of profound concern to our Community. The Nine vigorously condemn that system based on institutionalised racism and regret that it should be maintained in an authoritarian way in spite of clear cut disapproval and opposition. . . . The Nine stress that the persistence of that situation will entail a growth of tension, thus jeopardising the chances of an equitable and lasting solution.[17]

In another Communique, the policy of apartheid is described as 'immoral' and a 'violation of the fundamental human rights laid down in the UN Charter'.[18] The Community condemned the new constitution (1983) with its tricameral legislature and the establishment of independent homelands or bantustans. South Africa's military incursions into neighbouring states are viewed with hostility in Europe. A stream of demarches and statements has been issued regarding attacks on Angola, Lesotho, Mozambique, Botswana, Zimbabwe. In July 1985, the Foreign Ministers spoke of the 'existence of serious threats to the sovereignty and economic development of the states in Southern Africa'.[19] On the question of Namibia, the EC supports the implementation of UN Security Council Resolution 435 as a basis for the independence of that territory. Humanitarian demarches have been sent to the South African authorities regarding the plight of political prisoners and those awaiting execution.

According to the Foreign Ministers, the most fundamental issue facing the South African government is to 'initiate a dialogue with the genuine representatives of those South Africans now excluded from the present government structure'.[20] The plea for dialogue has been accompanied by a number of specific demands:

— the release of Nelson Mandela
— an end to detention without trial
— abandonment of the practice of forced removals
— removal of discriminatory legislation.[21]

The European Council at the Hague (June 1986) further called for a lifting of the ban on the ANC, the Pan Africanist Congress of Azania and other political parties because dialogue cannot take place without the presence of the recognised black leaders. Table 9 summarizes the EPC's stated policies towards South Africa.

Table 9
EC stated policy towards South Africa

* condemnation of apartheid
* condemnation of the state of emergency
* condemnation of detention without trial
* disapproval of the new constitution
* condemnation of the bantustan policy
* condemnation of attacks on neighbouring states
* support for UN Security Council Resolution (435) — Namibia
* calls for the release of political prisoners
* a lifting of the ban on political parties

The European Parliament The Parliament debated South Africa on many occasions during the 1980's and passed a long line of condemnatory resolutions. Such resolutions are usually based on the findings of background reports known as Working Documents drawn up by one or other of the Parliament's Committees. The Political Affairs Committee has responsibility for issues arising in political cooperation and therefore deals with South Africa; it receives opinions from other committees, notably, the Committee on Development Cooperation. The European Parliament is essentially a consultative body with the capacity to influence rather than to direct the course of EC policy. It exercises a control function vis-a-vis the Commission, and has the power to question the Council. Its budgetary powers enable the Parliament to propose new items of expenditure and to alter the provision of finance for certain categories of expenditure.

The Scott-Hopkins Report (1982) was the first global examination of Southern Africa by the Political Affairs Committee.[22] The resolution based on the report was passed by the Parliament on the 9 February 1982 by 130 votes to 96. The report examined the Community's only policy instrument of that time — the Code of Conduct — assessed the importance of South African exports of strategic raw materials, outlined EC policy towards the frontline states and dealt with policy towards Namibia. The tone of the report while condemning apartheid was conciliatory towards the Pretoria regime and did not call for an extension of the Community's policy instruments. The report did not call for sanctions. Support for the resolution came from a coalition consisting of the Conservative grouping, the Liberals and the European People's Party.[23]

Debates on South Africa have occurred with ever greater frequency during the last three years arising from the deteriorating situation in South Africa and growing international concern. In 1986, there were two important debates which responded to Community decisions taken at the Hague in June and in September by the Foreign Ministers. The July resolution was a very lengthy one and included statements on all facets of apartheid and the illegal occupation of Namibia. Guidelines were established for the use of monies allocated to positive measures to aid the victims of apartheid. It called on the Community to assist South Africa's neighbouring states (the SADCC countries) to become more independent of South Africa. The resolution laid considerable stress on the international dimension of policy towards South Africa, notably, the report of the Commonwealth Eminent Persons Group. It was critical of the steps taken by the Community at the Hague and the failure to implement the measures quickly.[24] The resolution was passed by 228 votes to 114 with 29 abstentions. Arising from technical difficulties the votes of individual MEP's were not recorded.

Following the adoption of punitive measures in September 1986, the Parliament debated South Africa during its October session. A number of political groupings initiated a debate by asking oral questions and requesting a debate. Five motions were tabled by the Liberal Grouping,[25] the European People's Party,[26] the Socialists,[27] the Communists,[28] and the European Right.[29] The latter was withdrawn and the Liberal motion was adopted without a vote. This motion called on the Member States to lend moral and material support to all South African organizations willing publicly to pledge themselves to a pluralist and non-racial democratic system.[30]

All groups in the European Parliament engage in the ritual condemnation of apartheid but significant differences arise concerning tactics and strategies for dealing with South Africa. The Socialist resolution which was passed by 200 for, 133 against and 24 abstentions[31], deplored the fact that coal was not included in the September 1986 package and urged the acceptance of such a ban, regretted the inadequacy of the measures, welcomed positive measures for the victims of apartheid and the passage of the US Anti-Apartheid Bill. The resolution considered that in the absence of UN mandatory measures, other ways should be found to develop a sanctions policy. Those Member States who had already adopted measures going beyond EC measures were commended and urged to go even further as an impetus for the achievement of a strengthened sanctions policy.[32]

The Communist resolution was most critical of EC policy and called for strong measures including a ban on new investment and new loans; a ban on the importation of minerals, textiles, agricultural products, and a ban on the export of computers and oil. The resolution which was passed by 166 votes to 160 with 4 abstentions considered that the immediate imposition of comprehensive sanctions is the only means of abolishing apartheid.[33] The EPP resolution took note of the September 1985 measures and wanted the remaining issue (coal) to be resolved in a satis-factory manner. It called on the Foreign Ministers to give an assessment of the effect of the boycott and to ensure that they were monitored properly.[34] The resolution was passed by 309 votes for, 11 against with 6 abstentions.[35]

The voting on these resolutions shows that the European Parliament now advocates a sanctions policy unlike the situation when the Scott-Hopkins Report was debated in 1982. The Socialists and Communists are most critical of Community policy and call for the strongest measures. The Liberals and the European People's Party adopt a middle course of favouring limited measures. The European Democratic Group (Con-servatives) highlight the importance of positive measures but offer no support for sanctions. The group of the European Right is totally opposed to sanctions and raises the spectre of a Communist takeover in South Africa. The group emphasises human rights violations in other countries, especially in Eastern Europe.

Irish MEP's have not been at all active in the Parliament on the ques-tion of South Africa; only six deputies out of fifteen voted on the October 1986 resolutions. Deputy Lalor was the only Fianna Fail member to cast a vote and was the only Irish MEP to intervene in the debate. He voted in favour of the Socialist motion. Deputies Banotti (FG), Clinton (FG) and O'Malley (FG) by voting in favour of this motion, broke with the Euro-pean People's Party (Christian Democrats) line. The EPP deputies voted against the Communist resolution calling for comprehensive sanctions. Table 10 outlines the voting pattern of Irish MEPs.

The votes by the Irish MEP's on the resolution is of some significance because there was a vote during the budget debate which sought to implement one of the demands of the October resolution, namely, a

Table 10
Voting in the European Parliament on South Africa
October 1986

	Doc B2-947/86 Resolution A (Socialists)	Doc B2-948/86 Resolution B (EPP)	Doc B2-951/86 Resolution C (Communists)
For	200	309	166
Against	133	11	160
Abstain	24	6	4
TOTAL	357	326	330
Irish MEPs			
For	Banotti Clinton Lalor O'Malley	Banotti Clinton Maher O'Malley Raftery	—
Against	Maher	—	Banotti O'Malley
Abstain	Raftery	—	—

Source: EP Proceedings, October Session 1986

call on the EC and its Member States to increase aid to the States neighbouring South Africa directly and through SADCC.[36] This is elaborated on in the section on the regional dimension of policy towards South Africa (page 71ff).

What is being done? In September 1977 after just two discussions, the Member States agreed to a Code of Conduct for Community firms operating in South Africa. The Code was intended to give teeth to the Community's oft-repeated condemnation of apartheid. In the UN the larger Community states had faced sustained criticism because of their economic involvement in South Africa and support for the apartheid economy. Barber claims that

the code was introduced as a political act prompted by the member governments anxiety to ward off international criticism. It was prepared quickly and pushed through the Council of Ministers to meet the timescale of the Lagos conference.[37]

At the UN Lagos anti-apartheid conference the Code was placed in the broad context of EC opposition to apartheid by the Belgian Foreign Minister speaking on behalf of the Community.

Because the Code was the first specific policy measure adopted by the Member States acting collectively, high expectations were placed on it. First, the Code had the social objective of improving the working conditions and terms of employment of black workers. It was anticipated that foreign investment by adopting enlightened employment practices could act as a force for change in South African society. Second, the Code would foster the elimination of apartheid. Gaston Thorn described the Code as part of the 'framework for the struggle against racial discrimination'.[38] The Code was revised in November 1985 as part of the positive measures adopted in September of that year.

Provisions of the EC's Code of Conduct November 1985 *Coverage*

---

1) *Relations Within the Undertaking:* The right of association, recognition of black trade unions, collective bargaining, information concerning the Code.

2) *Migrant Labour:* Employers have the social responsibility to contribute towards ensuring freedom of movement for black African workers, opportunities for them to lead a normal family life.

3) *Pay:* Special responsibility as regards pay and conditions of employment. Pay based on the 'supplemented living level' (data devised by the University of South Africa) considered as the absolute minimum necessary and should try to exceed this. Principle of equal opportunities and equal pay should apply.

4) *Training/Promotion:* Training for black employees, supervisory and management jobs open to black employees, no segregation in training.

5) *Fringe Benefits:* Living conditions — health, accident insurance, pensions, adequate medical care, education of family, accommodation, transport, leisure facilities.

6) *Desegregation:* Practices of segregation should be abolished — canteens, sports, training.

7) *Encouragement of Black Business:* Assistance to black employees to set up their own companies.

Source: Code of Conduct as revised by EC Foreign Ministers, 19 November 1985

The Code has been the subject of much debate since its inception in 1977. Its implementation is the responsibility of the Member States and one of its essential characteristics is its voluntary nature; there is no legal requirement on firms to adhere to the Code's provisions. In its favour, the Member State Governments claim that it has improved the employment practices of companies in South Africa. The Foreign Ministers described it as a 'useful instrument for the emancipation of Black workers'.[39] A European Parliament Report maintained that the Code has helped to establish racially mixed trade unions, has improved the lot of migrant workers, increased wages, and lessened racial segregation in the workplace.[40]

Critics of the Code argue that a proportion of companies were not paying the recommended wage levels in 1983-84; more than 10,000 black employees fell below the minimum wage urged by the Code.[41] A number of EC firms were refusing to negotiate with black trade unions and total desegregation of the workplace had not been achieved in all firms. Training opportunities were limited, the key to the advancement of black workers.[42] The Code applied to 175,000 workers, just two percent of the total black workforce. The monitoring of the Code is weak and there is no attempt to check the accuracy of the data supplied by the companies.[43]

The Code was and is politically useful to the Member States. It could be pointed to at the UN and other international fora while falling short of restrictive measures. It may have the adverse consequences, however, of supporting the status quo and of enabling foreign companies to remain in South Africa purporting to act as agents of change. It has been claimed that rather than promote change, the Code has stabilised the status quo, served to legitimise EC investment and to disarm anti-apartheid critics.[44]

A tentative move towards sanctions (1985) Consideration of African affairs in EPC was dominated by events in Southern Africa from 1984 onwards. With the deteriorating situation in South Africa, the industrialised countries were forced to consider policy options that went beyond cool diplomacy and rhetoric. In the United States, the European Community, the Commonwealth, and the Nordic Council the debate shifted to sanctions despite the instincts and official policy line of many of the major Governments concerned.

In August 1985, a troika of EC Foreign Ministers visited South Africa on a fact-finding mission. They met with the authorities and with representatives of the churches, the trade union movement, businessmen and leaders of various political organisations. The main purpose of the visit was to express to the South African Government the Community's concern 'at the lack of any specific progress towards abolishing apartheid'.[45] The visiting group concluded that the South African authorities were not committed to significant reform.

The Council of Foreign Ministers heard the report of the visiting group and after considerable resistance from some Member States, agreed to a series of measures that would come into force on January 1, 1986. These included:

— an oil embargo
— withdrawal of military attaches

— an embargo on the export and import of arms
— embargo on sensitive equipment destined for South Africa's security forces
— prohibition on new collaboration in the nuclear field
— agreement to discourage cultural, scientific and sporting contacts.

The UK refused to support the measures and maintained a reserve until September 25. The British Foreign Minister stated that the UK was 'firmly opposed to economic sanctions of any kind'. This package of restrictive measures amounted to a very minimal agreement among the Member States; most of the measures were already in place and merely conformed to well-established UN policy. The Communique stated that 'the question of other measures, including sanctions, remain'.[46] At the UN, the President-in-Office, declared that 'The Ten reserve the right to reconsider their position, if there is not significant progress within a reasonable period'.[47] The 1985 package was a signal to South Africa that the Community might feel obliged to take further action. The negotiations on the agreement allowed the participants to assess the positions of the various Member States on harsher measures.

The 1986 package In the first two months of 1986 there was increased activity on South Africa in all EC institutions arising from the need to develop a policy line for a number of important meetings

(1) EEC/ACP Joint Assembly, Swaziland, January 27-31
(2) South African Development Coordination Conference (SADCC) Zimbabwe 30-31 January.
(3) Meeting between EC Foreign Ministers and those of the Front-Line States, Lusaka, February 3-4.

These meetings afforded the African states ample opportunity to raise the question of South Africa and to press for stronger measures. The EEC/ACP Assembly served to highlight the issue for MEPs. The SADCC meeting which was attended by EC Development Ministers, although it concentrated on economic issues, had political undertones. The SADCC itself was established to improve the economic capacity of the 'frontline' states and to enhance their independence vis-a-vis South Africa. The political meeting between the Community Foreign Ministers and those of the frontline states was most significant because it established dialogue at the highest level. Trade sanctions proved to be the divisive issue of the meeting; President Kaunda of Zambia called for strong collective action and a reference to sanctions in the Communique. France, Greece, Ireland, Spain and Denmark were prepared to agree to this but the UK and Germany refused.[48]

The Dutch Presidency of the Council which began on the first of January 1986 placed South Africa high on its EPC agenda. The aim was for a harmonised EC approach and universal measures. A Dutch diplomat claimed that 'one small step with Twelve is better than big strides on our own'.[49] The Presidency set out to assemble an agreement on the issue among the Member States. As South Africa singularly failed to respond to repeated international pleas for change, pressure mounted in EPC for a coordinated response: meetings at Ministerial and expert level intensified. Numerous EP resolutions were passed calling for sanctions. An EPC meeting of the political directors in March 1986 issued a statement asking the South African authorities to release Nelson Mandela and to lift the restriction on political parties. The report of the Commonwealth Eminent Persons Group was published in June and concluded that the South African authorities were unwilling to negotiate. The South African Government announced the reimposition of a state of emergency.

The Dutch Presidency decided to propose a limited package of sanctions to a Ministerial meeting on June 16. The proposals were rejected by Britain, Germany and Portugal. South Africa then became the main issue of concern at the European Council meeting (June 26-27). A preliminary meeting of Foreign Ministers (26 June) highlighted the persistence of wide divergences on the issue. The proposed sanctions covered fruit, vegetables and wine at first; coal, steel and gold coin were added. The Netherlands, Ireland, Denmark, Greece and Spain strongly supported the measures. France, Belgium, and Luxembourg were willing to agree if the package was adopted by all. Chancellor Kohl remained firmly opposed. A face-saving device was fashioned. Sir Geoffrey Howe, the British Foreign Minister was asked to visit South Africa on behalf of the Community, in his capacity as President of the Council.

The Communique stated that:

> in the next three months, the community will enter into consultations with the other industrialized countries on future measures which might be needed covering in particular a ban on new investments, the import of coal, iron, steel, and gold coins from South Africa.[50]

Proposed measures covering fruit, vegetables and wine were excluded. Thus a process of diluting the package began from the outset. Both Prime Minister Thatcher and Chancellor Kohl claimed that the automatic implementation of the package could not be foreseen even if the Howe visit failed.

The Howe visit to South Africa essentially delayed the implementation of Community sanctions — it was an exercise in 'buying time'. Initially the visit was delayed because the South African authorities refused to meet him, as did Oliver Tambo, the leader of the ANC. Britain's Presidency of the Council and continued pressure from the Commonwealth led to a perceptible shift in UK policy. Mrs. Thatcher told the Commonwealth leaders in August that she would not block the Hague measures. At a press conference, Mrs. Thatcher claimed:

> They were bent on further action against South Africa in the genuine belief that only this would move President Botha, and so it was in that situation — our beliefs and their beliefs — that we decided first, that if

in the autumn, the European Community decided to introduce the measures mentioned in the Hague Communique . . . we would accept and implement them.[51]

Britain's Presidency greatly facilitated this change. By September, Herr Genscher, the German Foreign Minister indicated that he would agree because he was 'moved by the arguments that the EC could be damaged by further delay'.[52]

Although all of the Member States had by now indicated their willingness to adopt sanctions, the complete adoption of the Hague package did not materialise. The Foreign Ministers meeting of September 16-17 developed into a 36 hour marathon. Agreement was reached on the following measures:

> the Twelve should now proceed to adopt a package of restrictive measures on the lines envisaged at the Hague. This consists of a ban on new investment and on the import of iron, steel and gold coins from South Africa.[53]

It was the Hague package minus coal which represented 15 percent of South Africa's exports to the Community. Germany having finally agreed to sanctions was determined to restrict their impact and therefore refused to include coal as part of the agreement. Ireland, Greece and the Netherlands insisted that all of the Hague measures be adopted and even considered blocking the entire package because of the impact of minimal measures on the Community's credibility. Ultimately it was agreed that four measures were better than none; the Communique stated that coal would be included if consensus could be achieved at some future date.

Disagreement characterised the implementation of the package. Many countries favoured the adoption of the agreement by means of EC legislation but the UK and Germany feared the extension of the Community's competence. After numerous meetings, the measures dealing with steel were governed by ECSC law, gold coins by EC law and new investments by national measures under the framework of EPC. The ban on iron and steel proved to be weaker than at first thought. It did not cover ferromanganese, speciality steels, pipes and tubes. There were also problems concerning the date by which the measures should apply.[54]

The Hague measures: a tortuous path The debate on sanctions in EPC evolved with increasing intensity over a period of two years. Agreement on a minimal package of restrictive measures was fashioned slowly out of diversity. The Economist Intelligence Unit estimated that if the EC, US and Japanese measures were scrupulously implemented, South African exports in 1987 would be about 5 percent below what they might otherwise have reached.[55] Why the meagre results from the multiple rounds of negotiations on the issue?

Sanctions There is little support for a total embargo on trade with South

Africa among the Community countries: The EC states vote against the UN resolutions each year. Denmark is the only country that has passed a law prohibiting trade with South Africa (30 May 1986). On selective measures, the EC countries are divided between those states giving strong support to sanctions (Denmark, Ireland, Greece, and the Netherlands) and the 'hardliners' (UK, Germany and Portugal). France altered her stance on South Africa after the declaration of the State of Emergency in July 1985. From displaying little interest, France moved to an active policy position introducing a resolution on sanctions at the UN Security Council. The other Member States did not play a major role in these negotiations; they were willing to go along with the emerging consensus.

National diversity EPC involves a process of cooperation in foreign affairs involving twelve countries. On South Africa there was considerable divergence among the Member States in the period 1984–1986. Consensus is the dominant characteristic of collaboration in this area and the achievement of consensus on this issue took a long time. A combination of factors, notably, domestic pressure, international circumstances and the attitude of the other Member States forced the recalcitrant states to alter their positions. Those that favoured EC measures had to get the issue on the agenda and thereafter had to assemble an agreement. EPC has been likened to a convoy which moves at the pace of the slowest ship.[56] The hard bargaining and conflict which characterises the Council of Ministers is absent in EPC.

The economic dimension Germany as South Africa's major trading partner in the Community and the UK as the predominant investor had important economic interests at stake. This coloured their approach to sanctions from the outset. Both states are adamant in their opposition to restrictive measures. Their isolation within the Community forced them to soften their policy approach but even then Germany fought successfully to dilute the strength of the measures.

Size Size is an important factor in EPC. France, Germany and Britain constitute a significant 'inner core' in EPC by virtue of their size, economic power and military role. Italy is sometimes but not always regarded as a 'large state'. Diplomats from these countries consider themselves as 'serious countries' in foreign policy collaboration.[57] There is a tension in EPC between the larger and smaller states. Wallace (1983) points out that

> North-South issues in general, and South Africa in particular, have been points on which the larger states have felt themselves most constrained, criticized and even irritated by their smaller partners.[58]

The smaller countries have been active in calling for a strong Community line as the situation in South Africa deteriorated. The two large states managed to delay dealing with the issue for two years but ultimately had to succumb to internal and external pressure. France's adoption of an active approach strengthened the hand of the smaller countries as it served to highlight the maverick stance of the two large partners.

Domestic environment National governments have to consider the importance of an issue on the domestic agenda in taking foreign policy decisions. There are relatively influential anti-apartheid movements in Denmark, Ireland, the UK, and the Netherlands. Pressures of public opinion are weaker in Belgium, Germany, Luxembourg. Anti-apartheid groups in France, Italy, Greece, Spain and Portugal have little or no public impact.[59] The influential movements in the smaller countries have considerable impact on government policy in the absence of other countervailing economic pressures. The British movement has to contend with the strong economic interaction between the UK and South Africa and the undoubted influence of business interests on government policy. France's active approach may be explained by a combination of factors. First, France's economic interests in the region were limited. Second, France had everything to gain in terms of its relations with the rest of Africa from a strong anti-apartheid stance. Third, a Socialist Government facilitated the change.

Alliance considerations As the US Administration's policy of constructive engagement came under renewed pressure, the EC stance was the focus of world attention. The Hague Summit Communique specifically addressed the importance of consultation with the other industrialised countries.[60] The adoption of the US Anti-Apartheid Act in October 1986 highlighted the minimal nature of the Hague measures.

Positive measures The September 1985 agreement[61] was a twin-track one involving not just punitive measures but also positive measures to aid the victims of apartheid.

The programme is funded by a specifically created budget line (953) and 10m ECU was allocated in 1986 rising to 20m ECU for 1987. Responsibility for the programme was given to DG 8 (Development Cooperation) at the Commission because of its experience in dealing with non-governmental agencies. Most of 1986 was spent working out the structures for implementing the positive measures. It was decided to channel the funds through European non-governmental agencies to their partners in South Africa itself. The European NGO's therefore dealt with the Commission on behalf of the South African recipients. The Member States established a committee of national experts to keep a watching brief over the programme.

Four channels of aid were established

1. The Kagiso Trust
2. South African Council of Churches

3. South African Catholic Bishops Conference
4. Trade Unions

Positive Measures

— Code of Conduct: adaptation, reinforcement and publicity;

— Programme of assistance to non-violent anti-apartheid organisations, particularly to the churches;

— Programmes to assist the education of the non-white Community,
including grants for study at universities in the countries organising the measures;

— Intensification of contacts with the non-white community in
the political, trade unions, business, cultural and scientific, and
sporting sectors;

— Programmes to assist SADCC and the frontline states;

— Programmes to increase awareness among the citizens of the
Member States resident in South Africa.

Once the channels had been agreed to, attention was then paid to the
criteria for aid, priorities and procedures. The negotiations also included
discussion of the eligibility of Namibian projects for funding. Despite
the reservations of a number of the Member States this was agreed to.
Priorities for the programme include humanitarian aid, training and education, social support, legal assistance and advice. In addition to positive
criteria, a number of prohibitions on the use of aid were agreed to,
notably, funding could not be channeled to the South African authorities,
to the homelands and the so-called independent states. The projects
would have to promote unity among the peoples of different cultural,
ethnic and racial backgrounds. This latter criterion was intended to
prevent the flow of aid to Inkatha which under its leader Chief Buthelezi
promotes ethnic division.

Assessment of the positive measures is not possible given their recent
origin. In the short term, aid to the victims of apartheid helps to alleviate
the excesses of the regime and helps individuals who have fallen foul of
the system. In the long term, aid to the trade union movement will
strengthen the capacity of black workers to dismantle apartheid in the
workplace by using their economic power. Education and training are
important given the deleterious effects of 'bantu education'. Teachers
and lawyers are the most important professional categories required by
the black population.

The implementation of the project has been neither smooth nor automatic. Discussions on priorities and criteria were protracted and difficult
because of the sensitive nature of the programme. In April 1987, the
South African channels and their European partners actually suspended

implementation of the programme because of 'differences between themselves and the European Commission' concerning its implementation.[62] Difficulties related in the first instance to the interpretation of the initially agreed criteria for the acceptance of projects. The South African channels were insistent that they alone should decide on the projects for submission to Brussels. The Commission should be flexible with procedures given the special circumstances in South Africa. It was not always possible to give complete information regarding projects because of the danger to the participants from the security forces. Reporting procedures and mechanisms would have to take into account the risks to personnel in South Africa. In addition, the South African channels wanted to ensure that the political nature of the programme would be stressed. In other words, it was not simply a humanitarian programme but aimed at 'the transformation of South African society'.[63] It was feared that those countries opposing restrictive measures could use the 'positive' measures as a substitute for the former. A meeting on 2 June 1986 between the European Non-Governmental Organisations (NGOs) and the Commission clarified the issues that arose during the first year of the programme's life and the South African channels have agreed to resume submitting projects for the special programme.

At a meeting on 16 October 1986, representatives of the South African recipients of aid underlined the fact that they were dedicated to overcoming the apartheid system through non-violent means but said that they wanted a more active policy from the European Community.[64]

EPC at the UN Foreign policy cooperation extends into international fora, notably, the UN. The Member States meet on a weekly basis to exchange views, to consult and where possible to adopt a common voting position during sessions of the General Assembly. Cooperation extends to the workings of the main Assembly committees as well as the plenary sessions. There is considerable informal collaboration between the delegations. If one country receives a draft resolution from a non-EC state this will be circulated immediately so that the Member States can begin to fashion a response. The EPC process may lead to four types of activities in the UN:

— Joint Declarations on Agenda items
— Joint voting behaviour
— Joint Declarations concerning voting
— Letters and Communications to the Secretary General

The first and fourth diplomatic instruments are used extensively by the Member States. It is common practice for the President in Office of the Council to address the General Assembly on behalf of the Twelve.

The Member States attempt to go beyond declaratory diplomacy to common voting positions. Apartheid and Namibia were issues that demonstrated the limits to consensus among the Member States in the 1970's.[65]

Lindemann (1982) concluded that 'Denmark, the Netherlands and Ireland were more prepared than other EC states to agree to the demands of the developing countries'.[66] Foot (1979) argued that

> Denmark and Ireland often join together and vote differently from the other member states on many third world issues. On a number of occasions, these two states are joined by Holland and Italy to form what might be called a progressive voting block.[67]

The analysis of UN voting on apartheid during the 1980's in Chapter Two suggests that this trend has continued although Italy could not be placed in the 'progressive voting block' on apartheid. The accession of Greece (1981) and Spain (1986) has strengthened the progressive voting block on apartheid issues.

Agreement among the Member States on 'apartheid' resolutions is not prevalent. Out of a total of 70 votes between 1980 and 1986, joint voting only occurred on seven occasions (see Table 11).

Table 11
EC voting on apartheid resolutions 1980-1986

Year	Total Votes	EPC Agreement Joint Voting
1980	15	3
1981	14	2
1982	9	—
1983	10	—
1984	7	—
1985	8	1
1986	7	1
TOTAL	70	7

Source: Abstracted from Proceedings of UN General Assembly 1980–1986

The accession of Greece to the Community in 1981 partly explains this pattern. In a number of votes between 1982 and 1984, Greece was the only country voting against the others. Greece abstains on the resolution mentioning Israel but the other countries vote against. On the other issues the United Kingdom given its hardline stance, was the only country deviating from the majority position.

An overview of EC voting on apartheid resolutions during the 41st General Assembly (1986) highlights the absence of agreement on this issue among the Member States. Out of a total of seven votes, they voted together on just one occasion, divided into two groups for a further two votes and split three ways on four votes. Table 12 below lists the number of times a country was willing to go it alone, vote with the majority of EC countries or with a minority grouping.

Table 12
EC voting – 41st General Assembly 1986
apartheid resolutions

Country	No of Times Voted Together	No of Times in Majority Group	No of Times in Minority Group	No of Times Voted Alone
Belgium	1	6	—	—
Luxembourg	1	6	—	—
Germany	1	4	1	1
UK	1	3	1	2
France	1	5	1	—
Italy	1	6	—	—
Netherlands	1	5	1	—
Ireland	1	3	3	—
Denmark	1	3	3	—
Spain	1	4	2	—
Greece	1	2	2	2
Portugal	1	6	—	—

Source: Abstracted from UN General Assembly Proceedings, 1986

Only three countries (the UK, Greece, and Germany) were prepared to vote alone; the UK opposed two resolutions that the other countries either abstained on or voted in favour of, Greece supported two resolutions that failed to find favour with the other Member States. Belgium, Luxembourg, Italy, France, the Netherlands and Portugal voted with the majority on most occasions. Ireland and Denmark found themselves in a minority voting block on three occasions. This table shows that Greece, the UK, Ireland and Denmark were prepared to adopt voting positions at variance with the majority on numerous occasions.

Arising from the lack of consensus in EPC on South Africa, some countries develop a policy line with 'likeminded' West European and Third World countries. Lindemann (1982) observed that 'the smaller EEC states . . . seek concerted action with other likeminded countries in the General Assembly'.[68]

The resolution on 'Concerted International Action' is an example of collaboration beyond the confines of EPC. Eight of the smaller European states, including Ireland, co-sponsor this resolution together with a number of African states (p.45). In 1984 when the resolution was first introduced, Britain voted against and Belgium, France, Germany and Luxembourg abstained. Since then the EC countries co-sponsoring the resolution (Ireland, Greece and Denmark) have persuaded Belgium, Italy, France and Luxembourg to vote in favour. Britain continues to oppose the resolution and Germany abstains, demonstrating that the cleavage on sanctions runs through EPC activity at all levels.

Ireland rarely votes with the larger EC states on South Africa and is willing to go it alone or to vote in the minority voting block. The impact of EPC may be traced to a number of specific resolutions. In 1976, Ireland abstained on a resolution calling for a mandatory arms embargo against South Africa whereas, in previous years, Ireland supported this resolution. In 1976, the resolution mentioned German collaboration with South Africa: the FRG denied the allegations in the resolution and made representations to Ireland on the issue. As a result, Ireland altered its voting behaviour. Denmark had decided in EPC to abstain on the vote as well, but voted in favour because of the voting intentions of the other Nordic states. The change in policy with regard to comprehensive and mandatory sanctions (p.45) may have been influenced by the voting intentions of the other states. Ireland moved from a position of abstention to a negative vote in 1985 and 1986. All of the other states apart from Greece registered a 'no' vote.

The Regional Context

South Africa is the predominant military and economic power in Southern Africa and is the major trading partner for many of the 'frontline' states. The most pressing element of dependency is in the area of communications and transport. There is also considerable migration of labour from these states, particularly Mozambique and Lesotho, to South Africa. The latter has always used its economic power to extract political and diplomatic concessions from its neighbours.[69] South Africa has engaged in sustained and deliberate destabilisation of the region by using armed force against neighbouring states. They have all been the subject of one or more acts of aggression by the South African armed forces.

South Africa's economic domination, which would inevitably be a source of tension, is exacerbated by the apartheid nature of the regime and its occupation of Namibia. From 1977 onwards, the 'frontline' states (Angola, Mozambique, Botswana, Tanzania, Zambia and later Zimbabwe) discussed how they might reduce their dependency on South Africa. This culminated in the establishment of the Southern African Development Coordination Conference (SADCC) comprising the six 'frontline' states noted above in addition to Lesotho, Malawi and Swaziland.

The Lusaka Declaration (1980) outlined the major objectives of SADCC

1. reducing their level of economic dependency in general but in particular vis-a-vis South Africa
2. establishing links with a view to securing genuine and equitable regional integration
3. mobilising resources to promote the implementation of national, inter-state, and regional policies
4. taking coordinated action with a view to obtaining international co-operation in a strategy of economic liberation.

Each year SADCC holds a conference at which the major cooperating partner countries and international organisations pledge finance to priority SADCC projects. Of particular importance are projects to upgrade transport links between the various countries. The Beira Corridor is the most significant of SADCC's transport projects because it will join Zimbabwe, Zambia and Malawi to the Mozambique port of Beira. The need to strengthen the region's capacity to produce sufficient food is demonstrated by the famine in Mozambique. The promotion of investment in the region is one of the more recent priorities.[70] Dependence on South Africa is not something that can be overcome in a short time-span but will require decades of sustained regional cooperation and planning.

The SADCC Annual Report for 1986/1987 concluded that the total cost (adjusted for inflation) of South Africa's policy of destabilisation measured in terms of GDP lost was 30 billion dollars for the period 1980–1986.[71] Unless destabilisation is stopped, development cooperation finance will be spent on rebuilding what has been destroyed rather than on economic development in these countries.

All of the SADCC countries are now formally linked to the Community by means of the Lome Convention: Angola and Mozambique acceded to the Third Lome Convention (1985). Thus for the first time it becomes meaningful to talk of SADCC/EC relations. The Lome Convention pledges the support of the Community to ACP states that organise themselves into regional groupings and to step up their cooperation at regional and inter-regional level.[72] A proportion of the European Development Fund (EDF) is earmarked for regional projects. In addition, the EDF finances a development programme in each of the SADCC states. In the text of Lome III, apartheid is specifically mentioned in a declaration which includes a commitment on the part of the Community to work effectively for the eradication of apartheid.[73]

During the life of Lome I and II a large number of projects were financed in those SADCC countries that were part of the Convention. A combined total of 570.2 million ecu was channeled to SADCC countries from 1975 to 1985. (Appendix H provides a breakdown by country.) This amount will increase with the accession of Angola and Mozambique to the Convention. In addition to bilateral aid flows, a proportion of regional aid has gone to Southern Africa in the past. Eight percent of regional aid in Lome 1 went to projects in this region rising to 11 percent of aid in Lome II because of the participation of Zimbabwe in the convention. At a meeting of SADCC in January 1986, the first memorandum of understanding was signed between the EC and SADCC. A total of 110 million ecu was pledged over a five year period, 40 percent of which is destined for transport projects to SADCC as a region.[74] This formalised relationships between the European Community and SADCC.

A further 776 million ecu of Lome aid has been assigned to national indicative programmes in the nine SADCC countries. It has been argued that with ever increasing needs, particularly in the transport sector, the SADCC countries could effectively utilise regional resources well in excess of those allocated under Lome III (110 million ecu). Other major donors, notably, Canada, the Netherlands and the Nordic Group have made substantial increases to their regional programmes for the SADCC.[75]

Given the situation in the region, the annual pledging meetings held by SADCC have an important political dimension. A lessening of economic dependency on South Africa is politically important for the 'frontline' states because it will reduce South Africa's capacity to exploit this dependency for political ends. The first ministerial meeting between the leaders of the 'frontline' states and Community Ministers was held in January 1986. The institutions of Lome (Council of Ministers and Joint Assembly) provide a point of contact between EC representatives and the African countries. The SADCC countries place two essential demands before the EC. First, EC financial and technical aid is requested for development projects in the SADCC region. Second, the 'frontline' states despite the potential adverse consequences of sanctions for their economic well-being, call for harsh sanctions against South Africa. This request is made in the light of retaliatory action by South Africa against its neighbours.[76]

Meetings in all of the above fora discuss South Africa in one form or another. The EEC/ACP Joint Assembly (parliamentary tier) has a ritual motion of condemnation of South Africa at its twice yearly meeting. Since the first resolution in 1977, the framework for a policy has been developing. In 1977, the resolution merely stated that the EC must concern itself with the crisis in Southern Africa. Subsequent resolutions have been more detailed and have called on the Community to take punitive steps against Pretoria.[77] In 1985, a representative of the ANC was invited to address the Assembly. The EEC/ACP Resolution of 16 September 1986 deplored the exclusion of coal from the sanctions package, welcomed the positive measures but called for the EC and ACP states to 'impose stronger measures because the inadequacy of the package may lead the South African Government to doubt the Community's strength of purpose and could weaken the means adopted by other countries.' The resolution commended those Member States who had taken measures beyond present EC policy.[78]

In autumn 1986, the European Parliament attempted to use its budgetary powers to add a new item of expenditure to Chapter 95 of the EC budget. This expenditure (Article 954) was intended to compensate the 'frontline' states and SADCC for the consequences of South Africa's policy of destabilisation. A figure of 10 million ecu was included in the draft budget to create a *European Compensation Fund*. At its meeting on November 13, 1986, the EP failed to agree to these monies by a mere four votes (174 in favour, 178 against and 6 abstentions.)[79] An earlier resolution (October 1986) calling on the Community to increase aid to the states neighbouring South Africa was passed by the Parliament.

Eight Irish MEP's (Deputies Clinton, Lalor, Lemass, Maher, McCartin, O'Donnell, O'Malley, Raftery) voted against the resolution on Article 954 and Deputy Fitzgerald abstained. Deputies Clinton, Lalor and O'Malley had voted in favour of the earlier resolution calling on support for SADCC. Article 954 might not have gained acceptance in the Council but the Parliament missed an opportunity to force the Council to address this initiative.

The Policies of Other States

The policies of the EC countries are influenced not only by their domestic environments but by the approach of other countries and international organisations. The Commonwealth has ensured that Britain has to justify its policies in a forum with considerable representation from black Africa. The failure of the Commonwealth Eminent Persons Group (June 1986) made it more difficult for Britain to maintain its total opposition to sanctions. Nordic cooperation has acted as an alternative reference group for Denmark. The policy stance of the United States, given its special relationship with Western Europe, is an important source of influence.

The USA The Carter Presidency adopted a distant approach to the South African regime. The Reagan administration (1981) reviewed this and opted instead for a policy of 'constructive engagement'. The US sought to persuade the South African authorities to bring about gradual change to the apartheid regime. Direct criticisms of South Africa were muted. Extensive contact between the US Government and South African officials became the norm. 'Constructive engagement' was discredited by the continuing intransigence of the regime in South Africa. The domestic context of US policy too altered dramatically. Groups such as TransAfrica and the Free South Africa Movement made apartheid a major issue on the political agenda; a strong coalition favouring an active policy emerged.

The Reagan Administration attempted to forestall this coalition by agreeing to a series of limited measures in 1985. The issue remained on the agenda and in October 1986 the US Congress voted by an overwhelming margin to over-ride a Presidential veto of the *Comprehensive Anti-Apartheid Act.*[80] The Act contains a series of economic, political and diplomatic measures with the objective of 'helping to bring about an end to apartheid in South Africa and lead to the establishment of a non-racial, democratic form of government'.[81] The Act asserts that 'the situation in South Africa constitutes an emergency in international relations'.[82]

The economic measures included the following items and entered into force in October 1986

— embargo on coal, steel, uranium, aluminium, iron, agricultural products and textile imports.
— embargo on the export of oil, arms, ammunition.
— prohibition of all new US investments in and credit to South Africa.[83]

The Sullivan Code (1977) relating to the employment practices of US firms in South Africa is mentioned in the text. The legislation provides for expanded assistance to support education and training of black South Africans. The package was forced on the US administration against its will because of the strength of support for unilateral measures in the US Congress. It is much stronger than any restrictive measures adopted by South Africa's other major trading partners.

Nordic cooperation South Africa has been high on the agenda of Nordic Cooperation for many years. The Scandinavian states (Sweden, Norway, Finland and Denmark) have traditionally adopted progressive policies on North/South issues and, as noted in Chapter Two, favour strong condemnation of South Africa at the United Nations. As small states, these countries display a deep commitment to the UN system and the Charter. Their approach is that sanctions should be mandatory and passed by the Security Council. Pending global action, the Nordic Foreign Ministers adopted a *Nordic Programme of Action Against South Africa* in October 1985. The following measures were included:

— ban on new investments
— attempts to reduce trade with South Africa
— implementation of Security Council Resolution 558, 1984
— prohibition on the importation of Krugerrands
— prohibition of new contracts in the nuclear field
— embargo on the export of computer equipment that may be used by the armed forces or police in South Africa
— embargo on loans
— prohibition on the transfer of patents
— ban on commercial air service.
— further restrictions in the field of sports, culture and science
— assistance to SADCC
— assistance to the victims of apartheid

During 1986 the debate on South Africa continued. Denmark and Norway are in the process of adopting far wider measures on a unilateral basis. In May 1986, Denmark passed a law prohibiting all trade with South Africa. Exemptions from the law may last for only two years.[84] The actual implementation of the Bill may run into difficulties because of the Community's common commercial policy. The Norwegian Government introduced a Bill on the economic boycott against South Africa and Namibia (14 November 1986). This act goes further than any other West European state. Norway now advocates comprehensive and mandatory sanctions. Sweden because of its investments in South Africa and its trade was initially reluctant to go along with comprehensive sanctions. Pressure from its neighbours forced it to adopt a trade embargo in 1987.

Ireland and EC policy EC policy towards South Africa reflects the interests of the twelve Member States concerned. The process of policy-making in the EC, which is dominated by negotiations and coalition-building, is such that no country is likely to have its approach adopted. Rather, agreement is assembled out of diversity. Each country brings its particular concerns and pressures to the negotiating table. Size is an important dimension of the negotiating process; the larger Member States have a greater capacity to hold out against agreement than the smaller countries. Yet South Africa is one example of an issue where the smaller EC countries managed to get two of the large Member States to concede on the principle of economic sanctions.

It is possible to distinguish an Irish contribution to the development of policy towards South Africa in EPC. It is less easy concerning development cooperation policies under the Lome Convention and the special programme for the victims of apartheid. These programmes are implemented by the Commission with little involvement from the Member States once the ground rules have been established by the Council of Ministers. The process of political cooperation is where national approaches are most evident.

As apartheid is one of the traditional concerns of Irish foreign policy, Irish foreign policy makers took an active interest in the EPC working group on Africa. Ireland together with the Netherlands and Denmark favoured the development of an 'EC' approach to South Africa. From 1977 onwards, successive Irish Ministers sought a more active policy on South Africa and the emergence of collective measures. The Code of Conduct was frequently cited as an example of Community action and there was no public criticism of the Code from Irish politicians.

When in 1985 Community policy entered a state of flux, Ireland together with Denmark, the Netherlands, Greece and more recently Spain pressed for stronger measures. The 1985 package of restrictive and positive measures was regarded by Ireland's Foreign Minister, Mr. Peter Barry as a minimum and the Ten in their statement specifically referred to the fact that other measures, including sanctions remained on the table. The measures were designed to make clear in unambiguous terms, the seriousness with which the Ten viewed the situation in South Africa and the need for the abolition of the apartheid system in that country and the opening of a genuine dialogue with the representatives of the black majority population.[85]

Throughout the latter half of 1985, Ireland's involvement in EPC was complicated by growing pressure at domestic level for unilateral measures.

Ireland's foreign policy makers were hostile to 'going it alone' and placed all their faith in concerted action. Thus in an attempt to avert unilateral measures, the Minister for Foreign Affairs spoke again and again of forthcoming EC action and the search for agreement in Brussels. EPC seems to have been used as a cover facility and a means to deflect internal pressure. Yet in December 1985, a unilateral ban on the importation of fruit and vegetables was announced ahead of the EC partners. Once the political bargaining and negotiations at domestic level had produced the ban, Ireland's representatives began to use it as a source of leverage at Community level.

Conclusions

The Community's policy towards South Africa has evolved during two distinct periods. The period between 1976 and 1985 was characterised by declaratory diplomacy and an ineffectual policy instrument — the Code of Conduct. The latter given its voluntary nature and limited coverage was incapable of being a meaningful agent for change in South Africa but was valuable as a policy instrument to the Community. The Code enabled the EC to say that it was doing something with regard to South Africa. The pressure of events in South Africa from 1984 onwards meant that the largely symbolic policies of the period 1976–1985 were more difficult to sustain.

Criticism of the Community's stance from the ACP and 'frontline' states, resolutions at the UN and calls for stronger collective action from a number of the smaller Community states all combined to force a reappraisal of the Community's approach. The Member States moved tentatively towards restrictive measures. The first package (1985) must be regarded as a mechanism to buy time. The measures amounted to no more than what many of the Member States were doing anyway. Nevertheless, Britain felt unable to accept the package at the September 10 meeting of Ministers. This signaled the difficulties that would arise during 1986 as calls for sanctions intensified.

Economic interests and concerns dictated British and German policy.

Portugal because of the presence of a large Portugese population in South Africa was also reluctant to accept sanctions. British opposition to the Hague package (June 1986) was diluted during the summer. Having assumed the Presidency of the Council, Britain had to work towards a consensus in EPC. Germany and Portugal continued their opposition right up to the sanctions Council in September.

Having finally agreed to restrictive measures in principle, Germany sought to dilute the package. The exclusion of coal was a major blow to the credibility of the measures because it was by far the most significant item in the Hague package. The 1986 agreement must be viewed as a policy outcome representing the lowest common denominator among the Member States. Yet two of the largest Member States were forced to adopt a position on sanctions at variance with their stated preference. One of the most prolific scholars on EC/South African relations, writing in 1985, concluded that sanctions were an unlikely foreign policy choice because collective agreement within EPC on such a radical shift in policy was improbable.[86] This shift in policy did materialise although the agreed sanctions package was limited.

■ CHAPTER 4 ■

The Domestic Environment and Irish Policy towards South Africa

D iplomatic relations do not exist between Ireland and South Africa. Nevertheless, there are economic ties between the two countries which influence the choice of policy options. The purpose of this chapter is fourfold. First, the nature of economic inter-action between Ireland and South Africa is assessed. Second, unilateral measures adopted by Ireland are examined. Third, the implementation of UN resolutions by successive Governments is charted and fourth, Ireland's aid policy in Southern Africa is outlined.

The Economic Dimension

The total value of Ireland's trade with South Africa is difficult to deter-mine because of the existence of two very different sets of data. Ireland's official trade statistics underestimate the level of trade between the two countries because of the exclusion of commerce through the Shannon Industrial Estate, a free trade zone. Tables 13 and 14 provide both the

Table 13
Ireland's Trade with South Africa and Namibia, from Irish data,
1980—1986

Year	Imports £m	Share of Total	Exports £m	Share of Total	Balance £m
1980	11.68	.20	11.04	.26	− 0.64
1981	10.88	.16	21.76	.44	+ 10.88
1982	13.42	.19	23.77	.41	+ 10.35
1983	12.92	.17	31.94	.46	+ 19.02
1984	17.36	.19	38.75	.43	+ 21.39
1985	20.40	.21	29.55	.30	+ 9.15
1986	16.19	.17	30.19	.32	+ 14.00

Source: Trade Statistics of Ireland, CSO 1980-86, Central Bank Annual Reports 1980—1986

Table 14
Ireland's Trade with South Africa, from South African data, £m (a)
1980–1985

Year	Imports	Exports	Balance
1980	13.18	33.21	+ 20.03
1981	25.24	37.07	+ 11.83
1982	30.80	35.20	+ 4.40
1983	39.67	43.90	+ 4.23
1984	43.35	45.56	+ 2.21
1985	31.15	39.92	+ 8.77

Source: South African Trade Statistics (1980–1985)
Note: (a) Calculated on the basis of the rand value (yearly average)

Irish and South African trade figures. The Irish figures suggest that the value of trade has increased significantly in the period 1980-1986. Exports reached a high of £38 million in 1984 and amounted to £30 million in 1986. In 1986, exports to South Africa represented only 1.7 percent of total exports to areas other than the EC, the USA and Canada and only 0.3 percent of total trade was conducted with South Africa.[1] South African trade statistics suggest that South African exports to Ireland are much higher than Irish trade figures indicate and that South Africa has a trade surplus rather than vice versa.

Two types of commodities dominate Ireland's imports from South Africa: fruit and vegetables and coal. Table 15 lists those products with an import value of more than £1 million in 1985.

Table 15
Categories of imports from South Africa with value over £1 million 1985

Product	£m	% of Total Imports from South Africa
Fruit and Vegetables	5.34	26
Coal	4.98	24
Fertilisers and Minerals	2.36	12
Textiles	1.48	7
Iron and Steel	1.33	6.5
Sugar and Sugar Preparations	1.19	6
Manufactured metals	1.19	6

Source: Trade Statistics of Ireland, CSO 1985

As both fruit and vegetables and coal have featured in the sanctions debate, Appendices I and J provide data for trade in these products between 1980 and 1986. Fruit and vegetables declined from 48 percent of total imports in 1980 to 23 percent in 1986. Coal on the other hand increased from 6 percent in 1980 to 18 percent in 1986.

Not only has the value of Ireland's fruit and vegetable imports from South Africa been declining, the importance of this source of supply has fallen from almost six percent of imports in 1980 to two percent in 1986. Coal on the other hand has increased from 1.1 percent in 1980 to 1.8 percent in 1986; the figure of 3.5 percent in 1985 arises because of the miners' strike in Britain.

Exports to South Africa consist mainly of organic chemicals, office equipment and pharmaceuticals. Table 16 lists those products with an export value of over £1 million in 1985.

Table 16
Categories of exports to South Africa with value over £1 million 1985

Product	£m	% of total Exports to South Africa
Office Machines	7.11	24
(Computers)	(5.87)	—
Organic chemicals	7.03	24
Pharmaceutical products	3.27	11
Machinery and equipment	1.47	5
Food	1.46	5
Manufactured metals	1.31	4
Scientific equipment	1.23	4
Misc. manufactured products	1.06	3.5

Source: Trade Statistics of Ireland, CSO, 1985

Ireland's exports of computer products to South Africa have increased in value from £0.08 million in 1980 to £8 million in 1986 (Appendix K provides figures for the export of this product for each year in the period 1980-1986.)

The figure of £8 million for 1986 shows a particularly sharp increase on the 1985 amount. However, the sale of computers to South Africa constitutes less than one percent of total exports of this product and therefore could not be considered vital for the viability of the firms concerned.

Trade with South Africa was not a political issue in Ireland during the 1960's. The Minister for External Affairs Mr. Frank Aiken, spoke of 'constantly pressing the South African authorities to take steps to secure a better balance in our trade with that country'.[2] By 1970, however, Coras Trachtala was instructed by the Government that no trade mission should be sent to South Africa and no official trade delegations received here. Notwithstanding this, the value of trade has continued to increase over the last two decades.

Investment is the other pillar of economic interaction. The flow of capital from Ireland to South Africa appears minimal. Irish individuals resident in South Africa could well have assets in South African banks arising from emigration. Portfolio investment which undoubtedly exists would be extremely difficult to trace.[3] Irish banks are involved in financing trade with South Africa by providing credit facilities for companies. Money has been lent to South Africa, through a banking syndicate, by the Bank of Ireland but the amounts involved are small. In reply to a Dail Question[4] Mr. John Bruton provided data on the assets and liabilities of the licensed banks vis-a-vis South Africa (Table 17).

Table 17
Assets and liabilities of Irish banks with South Africa £m

	Liabilities	Assets
1983 (end December)	5.8	1.0
1984 "	5.8	0.4
1985 "	4.8	0.1

Source: Dail Debates 361:2864, 18 February, 1986

The Bank of Ireland has declared its intention not to lend to South Africa again. The Allied Irish Bank had already adopted this policy line.

The flow of South African capital to Ireland is much more central to the debate on policy options. Large South African companies such as Anglo-American Corporation and the Rembrandt Group have equity shares in companies which in turn have interests in Irish companies, most notably, Carroll Industries, Beamish and Crawford, J. S. McCarthy and Cape Insulation.[5] Indirect investment of this nature does not however impinge all that directly on the concerns of Government. Direct investment in manufacturing industry looms large. Two South African companies, De Beers and Boart Hardmetals are located in the Shannon Industrial Estate. De Beers, the largest diamond mining company in the world, established its plant in Shannon in 1960, making it the oldest company on the estate. It employs a staff of approximately 700 and is engaged in manufacturing industrial diamonds. The Shannon plant acts as a clearing house for industrial diamonds manufactured in South Africa and Sweden as well as at Shannon itself. Boart Hardmetals is also one of the earliest companies to arrive in Shannon and employs 250 people. This plant manufactures percussion, mining and quarrying equipment. These two companies employ almost 1,000 people which represents over 20 percent of the total workforce on the estate. Moreover, these enterprises are regarded as anchor companies on the estate.

Attitude to Sanctions

Ireland as a trading nation places a high premium on conditions that help maintain reasonably free trade. The imposition of economic sanctions against any country including South Africa is seen as a measure of last resort. During the 1960's there was no support for the use of sanctions against South Africa; again and again in the Dail, the Minister for External Affairs, maintained that sanctions would hinder rather than help in ending apartheid. The difficulties that were experienced with sanctions in the 1930's were quoted.[6] Respect for the UN Charter and the role of the Security Council meant however that in the event of global action, Ireland would support the Security Council.[7] Major responsibility was vested in the larger trading nations. In 1969, the Minister for External Affairs maintained in the Dail that:

> Economic sanctions to be effective would need to be observed by the major trading countries and they have not been prepared to adopt such sanctions. While that remains the position, I feel we would not be justified in depriving our exporters and workers of the fruits of the market.[8]

Ireland is influenced by those countries with extensive economic ties with South Africa.

The aftermath of the Soweto rising in 1976 brought the question of sanctions against South Africa to the forefront of the agenda. Support for concerted international action through the UN became the central theme of Ireland's approach. The Minister for Foreign Affairs, Mr. Brian Lenihan said in the Dail in 1977 that Ireland favoured universal economic sanctions.[9] A ban on new investments and an oil embargo were favoured by successive Irish Governments. Selective measures rather than comprehensive sanctions received support. A Private Member's motion tabled by the Labour Party in the Dail (1981) which called 'upon the Government to take steps to introduce an immediate and effective boycott on all commercial and trading links with South Africa' was amended by the Government.[10]

A unilateral measure Given a well established and consistent policy line which called into question the effectiveness of unilateral measures, why then did Ireland introduce a unilateral ban on the importation of fruit and vegetables from South Africa in 1985? The answer lies in a strike that was as far-reaching as it was unexpected for the Government. What is widely known as the Dunnes Stores' strike began in July 1984 when Mary Manning working at a Dublin branch of the company, refused to check out two South African grapefruit for a customer on the grounds that she was following the guidelines issued by her union, the Irish Distributive and Administrative Trade Union (IDATU). She was suspended by management and following a breakdown in talks a picket was placed on the shop. A strike began which was to last over two years and which was to receive extensive media coverage in Ireland and abroad.

The strike raised a number of industrial relations issues, notably, the right of workers to refuse to handle goods on grounds of conscience. It also raised problems for the company if it were forced to introduce a unilateral ban while its competitors did not. Because of the protracted nature of the strike and considerable public sympathy with the strikers, the Minister for Labour referred the dispute to the Labour Court for consideration. In May 1985, the Court produced a report for the Minister which suggested that

— there should be an immediate return to work
— there should be a conference of major supermarket chains to agree to a voluntary code of practice designed to minimise the sale of South African goods in supermarkets
— discussions should be held between the social partners concerning the rights of conscientious objectors in employment.[11]

The workers refused to return to work until issues relating to the handling of goods were resolved. Notwithstanding this, discussions were held with the major supermarkets who gave a positive declaration of their intention to minimise the sale of South African produce.[12] Talks on the question of conscientious objectors in employment were not at all successful. The strike continued with mounting pressure on the Government to do something to resolve it.

During the first year of the strike, Cabinet involvement in the issue was minimal. The Minister for Labour, because it was an industrial relations dispute, tended to take the lead. In June 1985, the Minister, Mr. Ruairi Quinn announced his intention to propose to Cabinet a licencing system to restrict and minotor South African imports.[13] For the next six months the issue of a unilateral ban on the importation of fruit and vegetables was on the governmental agenda. The Government decision of December 1985 which announced the intention to adopt a unilateral stance was the result of protracted bargaining and disagreement among the Government departments concerned and in Cabinet. It took a long time to assemble the elements of the final package.

In June 1985, the Minister for Labour, Mr. Ruairi Quinn, circulated a discussion document to his colleagues in Cabinet outlining a proposal for the imposition of a licencing system for the importation of fruit and vegetables. The issue was brought to the Cabinet table not as a formal agenda item but as a subject for discussion. Proposals of this nature would normally be processed by the Departments of Foreign Affairs and Industry and Commerce, in the first place. However, any Cabinet Minister is free to introduce items for discussion if they are of special interest to him. From the outset the departments with responsibility for this policy area were not totally in control of the management of the dossier. The proposal to introduce a ban was at variance with the well established and frequently reiterated policy line regarding unilateral policy measures. How therefore was this policy stance changed?

Following the informal discussions on a ban in June 1985, the Department of Foreign Affairs was asked to make a submission to Cabinet on the issue — it was thus asked to examine a policy line to which it was fundamentally opposed. It is necessary to unravel the political and bureaucratic debate that ensued between June and December 1985 in order to establish how the unilateral ban came into being. A number of reservations were raised in the debate.

First, there was the longstanding policy which favoured concerted action rather than unilateral measures when using economic policy instruments. Second, there was the question of Ireland's obligations under international law. In the Dail, the Minister for Foreign Affairs, Mr. Peter Barry specified the provisions of Ireland's treaty obligations under the GATT and the Rome Treaty that would be broken if Ireland were to impose a unilateral ban on trade with South Africa. Given the importance of this consideration in the bureaucratic and political debate, the entire answer is quoted below.

A unilateral ban on trade with South Africa would conflict with the State's obligations under Article 113 of the Rome Treaty establishing the European Economic Community and under Articles 30 to 36 of the same Treaty, unless the measures imposing the ban could be justified by reference to a permitted derogation from the general rules on the grounds of public morality, public policy or public security. Such a ban would offend against Article XI of the General Agreement on Tariffs and Trade unless it could be justified by reference to a permissible derogation on specified grounds, for example, public policy or security.[14]

In reply to a related question on 5 December 1985, the Minister said that Ireland was not intending to seek a derogation under any of the let-out clauses and that what Ireland wanted was 'Community action or world wide action'.[15] Third, fears would have been expressed concerning precedent. If Ireland adopted unilateral measures in relation to South Africa, could this not be used to pressurise Ireland into a similar action again. Fourth, there would have been fears that South Africa might initiate proceedings against Ireland in GATT or that an individual trader could initiate proceedings in the European Court of Justice. Fifth, the employment of almost 1000 workers in Shannon in South African-owned companies was an important constraint in assessing unilateral measures.

Notwithstanding these objections or doubts, the Government agreed to a licencing system in December 1985 'given the *prima facie* case that the use of prisoners for farm labour was a common practice in South Africa'.[16] There were therefore a number of other factors that influenced Government. During this period representations were made to the Taoiseach Dr. Garret FitzGerald by the Irish Congress of Trade Unions (ICTU), Trocaire and the Irish Commission for Justice and Peace which favoured a unilateral ban on fruit. On 19 October 1985 Trocaire and the Irish Commission for Justice and Peace issued a joint statement on the question of sanctions.

> We are convinced that the situation is now such that Ireland should move decisively, without delay, to introduce sanctions on a progressive basis, beginning with a ban on imports of South African agricultural produce. The combination of moral, political and practical reasons in favour of this are collectively very strong.[17]

On 29 October a delegation from Trocaire and the Irish Commission for Justice and Peace met with the Taoiseach. In a statement issued by the delegation after the meeting, the question of GATT is raised. It is argued in the statement that while the imposition of sanctions might constitute a technical breach of GATT, compliance with GATT regulations could not be justified in the face of the enormity of apartheid and the effects of this policy on the people of South Africa. The statement goes on to say that countries such as Australia and the US which had imposed sanctions on South Africa had not been the subject of a South African complaint to GATT and that no aggrieved state had ever been awarded compensation by GATT arbitrators.[18]

The Irish Congress of Trade Unions wrote to the Taoiseach on 29 July 1985, and again, on 6 September calling on the Government to impose a ban on selected South African imports.[19] This request was reiterated in a meeting between the Taoiseach and a delegation from Congress held on 20 November 1985. Congress argued that such a move would provide psychological support for the black workers in South Africa and would be a symbolic token of Ireland's solidarity with them.[20] The Labour Court which had intervened in the strike for a second time in Autumn 1985, concluded that there was no real industrial relations solution to the strike in the absence of 'action of a political nature, for example, changes in the Unfair Dismissals Act or a ban on the importation of fruit and vegetables or a licencing system'.[21]

A legal device was found to overcome the reservations concerning Ireland's international commitments which were central to the debate. A legal opinion by the Attorney General, the Cabinet's source of legal advice, maintained that under GATT rules (Article XXe) a country could refuse to import produce if prison labour is used. Sweden had introduced a ban on the importation of agricultural produce earlier in 1985 and had cited this clause.[22] Apparently, the Attorney General argued that this let out clause would ensure that infringement proceedings would not be taken against Ireland under GATT rules.[23] Concerning the EC's common commercial policy, Ireland could well make a case under Article 36 relating to public policy. In any event it was unlikely that the Commission would take Ireland to the Court of Justice given that it had been highly critical of the apartheid regime in a statement issued in 1985.

During all this time the responses of the international community to events in South Africa were in a state of flux. In the absence of global measures many countries were deciding to go it alone or in concert with a limited number of countries. The Nordic Council had agreed to a series of measures as had the Commonwealth. The Reagan Administration, in an attempt to prevent the introduction of widescale sanctions by Congress, agreed to a series of limited measures. The European Community had in September introduced its first package of restrictive and positive measures which were regarded in Ireland as a minimum. Beginning in 1985, more and more countries were opting for sanctions in their policy towards South Africa. This meant that Ireland would not be alone in the event of unilateral measures being adopted.

Given the traditional objections to unilateral measures reiterated in the Dail on 5 December 1985, it is possible to conclude that the Government decision of 19 December which announced a unilateral ban was taken against the advice of the lead department in this policy area. The ban was therefore a most unusual foreign policy decision in that Cabinet opted for a policy line at variance with the expert advice. A number of factors explain this. In Cabinet the four Labour Party ministers favoured the measures given that Labour Party policy calls for 'the imposition of all-round sanctions against South Africa — economic' (including oil, military, sporting and diplomatic restrictions).[24] The Minister for Labour was very committed to solving the Dunnes Stores strike which commanded such widespread attention. A number of ministers including the Taoiseach were or had been associated with the Anti-Apartheid Movement. From the outset, the issue was not contained within the usual boundaries of foreign policy making. There was considerable domestic pressure on the Taoiseach and on the Cabinet. South Africa was high on the agenda of international politics and receiving constant media attention. Other countries were moving towards unilateral measures.

Although a decision in principle was taken in December 1985 on the fruit and vegetables ban, a verification process of the use of prison labour was required. In January 1986, an Amnesty International report was produced by one of Ireland's Professors of Law, Kevin Boyle, which served to strengthen the case for a ban. In addition the Minister for Labour, Mr. Ruairi Quinn pointed out in a letter to the Development Cooperation Committee of the Oireachtas that 'the necessary verification process can rely on studies of the living and working conditions of South

African workers which have already been undertaken by international organisations such as the I.L.O. to sustain the view that convict labour is extensively employed in South African agriculture'.[25] In March 1986 the Government announced its intention to licence the importation of South African fruit and vegetables from 1 October 1986 and to impose a total ban as and from January 1987. The decision to licence imports as a prelude to a total ban was to enable Fruit Importers of Ireland, who imported over 90 percent of total fruit imports from South Africa, to fulfil their contractual agreements and find alternative sources of supply. In evidence to the Joint Oireachtas Committee on Cooperation with Developing Countries, Fruit Importers maintained that although 'there is a bad political situation in South Africa . . . something similar could be said of other producing areas such as Chile, Argentina, Brazil, Philippines and Greece, also East European countries including Hungary and Poland'.[26] In other words, Fruit Importers saw no difference between human rights abuses in these countries and apartheid. A statutory order was issued on 14 August 1986 entitled Restriction of Imports (agricultural produce from South Africa) Order 1986.[27]

Once political agreement had been reached on the fruit and vegetables measures, politicians began to use the unilateral measures in a European context. As early as January 1987, the Minister for Labour maintained in a letter to the Chairperson of the Development Committee of the Oireachtas that

> The form of action decided upon by the Government before Christmas has placed Ireland in the forefront of action being taken by the European Community against South Africa. The Government will be informings its EEC partners of the action it proposes to take and will seek to bring them along with us in concerted action against South Africa.[28]

In July 1986, George Birmingham as Minister of State at the Department of Foreign Affairs claimed in the Seanad that the unilateral measures should be seen as 'an integral part of Ireland's national policy. That policy is among the most forward of western countries; Sweden and Norway only have announced similar restrictions on produce imports, while Denmark intends to prohibit all imports from South Africa'.[29] The Minister further claimed that 'the truth of the matter is that leadership within the Community on this issue has been provided by Denmark and Ireland'.[30] By this stage the unilateral measures were seen as useful leverage within EPC although the decision could not be regarded as an active and deliberate decision by the policy makers in Foreign Affairs. Rather it was the product of considerable domestic pressure, the symbol of the strike and the tardy nature of EC action.

Although it is too early to judge the effectiveness of the unilateral ban there is some evidence that sanctions busting may be occurring. There have been allegations that the Irish market is receiving South African fruit and vegetables via Swaziland.[31] Analysis of Irish imports of fruit and vegetables

July 1984	Strike begins in Dunnes Stores branch	
May 1985	Labour Court Report (1st)	
June 1985	Quinn statement re measures	
September 1985		EC positive and negative measures Swedish ban Nordic
October 1985	Second Labour Court Report Trocaire/Irish Commission for Justice and Peace Meeting with the Taoiseach	
November 1985	Meeting of ICTU with Taoiseach	
January 1986	Amnesty International Report on Prison Labour	
February 1986	IAAM submission on the legal case for sanctions	
March 1986	Government announces measures	
May 1986		Danish measures announced
June 1986		Canadian measures
October 1986	Implementation Phase I	US measures
November 1986		Norwegian measures
January 1987	Total ban on the importation of fruit and vegetables.	

from Swaziland since 1948 show a steady increase in 1984-86 and a sizeable increase for the first ten months of 1987 (see Table 18).

Ireland imported more fruit and vegetables (£0.495m) from Swaziland in September 1987 than it did for all of 1985 and the combined total for September/October 1987 (£0.893m) is more than the total for 1986 (£0.624m). Swaziland is one of the smallest countries in Africa surrounded by South Africa and heavily dependent on it. It has expressed opposition to economic sanctions against South Africa and the Ministry of Commerce there has alleged that certain South African businessmen are attempting to use the country as an illicit conduit for the export of South African goods.[32] It is questionable whether Ireland's imports of £2.39m could

In the above box after November 1985 insert:
December 1985 — Government announces measures subject to verification.
Line 1: For 1948 read 1984.

Table 18
Ireland's imports of fruit and vegetables
from South Africa and Swaziland 1984–1987 (£'000)

Country	1984	1985	1986	1987 (Jan–Oct.)
South Africa	5,447	5,340	3,707	–
Swaziland	227	355	624	2,391

Source: Trade Statistics of Ireland 1984–1987, CSO
Figures for September–October 1987 supplied by phone from CSO

have been supplied by Swazi production. The matter has been taken up with the Department of Agriculture by the Anti-Apartheid Movement.

The arms embargo Ireland implements the Security Council's mandatory arms embargo (1977). As Ireland does not manufacture arms, the main issue concerns 'grey area' products, notably, computers. During the 1980's, Ireland's exports of computers to South Africa increased steadily and amounted to over £8 million in 1986. Licences (import/export) are required for trade in certain goods to and from certain countries by Ireland. Orders made under the *Control of Exports Act (1984)* require licences for trade with South Africa. To obtain licences certain information and certain undertakings are required by the Department of Industry and Commerce. Although it is not a member, Ireland adheres to the COCOM (Coordinating Committee for Multilateral Export Controls) list of strategic commodities which cannot be exported to the Eastern block. An Irish exporter of these products must indicate a *final destination.* The export of computers to South Africa is subject to licence which is granted on the production of a statement from the *ultimate consignee* that the equipment will not be used by or sold to the security forces in South Africa. Licences for South Africa are valid only for three months; the norm for the other countries is six to twelve months.

Although there is no evidence that the security forces are in fact getting Irish products, it is virtually impossible to monitor these exports. There is the added problem of trade through a third country. If goods of Irish origin are exported to Britain or any other country, it becomes the responsibility of the third country authorities to regulate further trade in these products. It has been claimed although never proven that Digital in Galway supplied mini-computers to Plessey, a British company, which in turn used the computers in a mobile radar system it sold to South Africa.[33]

Other measures Over the years public agencies have been directed by successive Governments to refrain from contact with South Africa. There was never a comprehensive Government decision taken by Cabinet, rather individual Ministers and departments have periodically instructed their state-sponsored bodies to observe official policy towards South Africa. Aer Lingus and Bord Failte closed their South African offices in 1970. The ESB does not purchase South African coal for its generating stations, the IDA will not grant-aid South African companies and Coras Trachtala does not promote trade. Irish Shipping carried goods to and from South Africa until the demise of the company in 1984. This brought to an end the remaining contact between an Irish state company and South Africa. From time to time questions are raised concerning sponsorship of sporting events and conferences that may include South African partic-ipation; Aer Lingus and Bord Failte are the most frequently cited in this regard.

A circular was issued by the Minister for Health in September 1984 and again in October 1986 concerning economic interaction between health agencies in Ireland and South Africa. The Health Boards are major purchasers of food and medical equipment. The first circular asked all health agencies to ensure that 'no health agencies purchase items of South African origin or engage in commercial and other dealings with South African agencies'.[34] The circular was sent at the request of the then Minister for Health, Mr. Barry Desmond.

Visas Ireland is one of four EC countries (the others being UK, Germany and Greece) that do not require South African visitors to hold a visa. In return, Irish citizens do not require a visa for entry to South Africa. In 1982, the Dail was informed that the Departments of Justice and Foreign Affairs were examining the issue with a view to introducing visa arrange-ments.[35] This review took three years. Questions were asked in the Dail when the South African Ambassador to London, Mr. Denis Worrall visited Ireland in May 1985 and when the Dunnes Stores' strikers were refused entry to South Africa despite the no-visa requirement. The main issue relating to visas was the implications of any change for 'Irish nationals living in South Africa and retaining Irish passports . . . and Irish nationals visiting or travelling in transit through South Africa, including our Aid workers in Lesotho'.[36] Foreign Affairs and Justice concluded that the introduction of a visa regime would be counterproductive, as it would affect the aid programme in Lesotho.[37] The difficulties would arise because the aid programme is labour intensive and there are approximate-ly one hundred aid workers in Lesotho. They travel through South Africa to get to Lesotho and on occasion purchase spare parts for machinery in South Africa which are unavailable from another source. Furthermore products from the Lesotho craft industries are sold in South Africa.

Sport The UN embargo on sporting links with South Africa is one of the longest standing measures used in the fight to eliminate apartheid. It is important in the South African context because the white population are devoted to all forms of sport. During the 1960's the potential pressure that an embargo could exert was not realised in Ireland. In 1965, the Taoiseach Mr. Sean Lemass said in reply to a Dail question concerning the attendance of a Minister at a rugby match involving South African players, 'I do not see how attendance at an international football match could imply any point of view regarding the policies of the Governments of the countries concerned'.[38] This statement would not be made today by an Irish politician because of the sensitivity of South Africa as an issue.

By 1973, the Government informed all sporting organisations of the terms of UN resolutions on sporting contacts. Cospoir, the National Sports Council, adopted a policy line of withholding grants to bodies that maintain links with South Africa. This is the only form of direct control that the Government can use. The imposition of a visa requirement was used in 1979 to prevent the visit of a South African rugby tour to Ireland. In 1978 when it appeared as if Aer Lingus might sponsor a Tug-O'-War Championship involving a team from South Africa, considerable pressure was brought to bear on the organisers of the event. A visit by the Irish rugby team to South Africa in 1981 was the most controversial of all sporting issues in recent times. Throughout 1980, the Government made its opposition to the proposed tour well known. The Irish Rugby Football Union (IRFU) decided to accept the invitation regardless of the views of the Government, all political parties in the Oireachtas, the Trade Union movement and Church leaders.

The tour was discussed repeatedly in the Dail in the form of Dail questions and a Private Members Motion. Anger was expressed at the decision of the IRFU to tour as an Irish team despite strongly voiced opposition. Deputy Quinn in introducing the Private Members' Motion spoke of a sense of outrage that 'a team of rugby players bearing the Irish emblem and carrying the name of being an Irish representative side should represent in a most extended way any Irish citizen in a country which perpetrates injustice in a comprehensive fashion which makes it unique among the nations of the world'.[39]

The Government opposed the tour on a number of grounds. First, the tour was regarded as a breach of the Olympic principle of non-discrimination in sport. Second, there were fears that the tour might damage Ireland's international reputation especially with the Third World.

The Government was unwilling to revoke the passports of those intending to travel with the tour but did refuse leave to all potential players in public employment. As a result of the tour, the IRFU was refused grants for its activities. In order to minimise the negative impact of the visit on relations with the Third World, the Government was careful to publicise its opposition in the UN and with the Committee for the Abolition of Apartheid. Although the tour did in fact take place, the

debate in Ireland on apartheid had the effect of raising general consciousness of the inequities of the South African state.

The Oireachtas and Political Parties

It has not proved possible to get a comprehensive overview of the
attitudes of the various political parties on South Africa. All advocate a
policy of opposition to apartheid but differ somewhat on policy options.
Both the Labour Party and the Workers Party have produced policy
documents outlining party policy on this issue. In July 1982, the Administrative Council of the Labour Party when adopting their policy
document called for full economic, military, sporting and diplomatic
sanctions.[40] The Workers Party called for a full trade embargo against
South Africa in response to the ban on agricultural produce.[41] This was
followed in July 1986 by a call for a ban on South African coal.[42] In
response to the EC measures of September 1986, the Workers Party
advocated unilateral Irish measures and are particularly concerned with
the sale of computers to South Africa.[43] The Progressive Democrats
(PDs), a relatively new party, has not produced a policy document on
South Africa. It supported the adoption of the unilateral measures in
1986 and favours concerted EC and UN measures.

The two main parties (Fianna Fail and Fine Gael) support restrictive
measures but generally favour global rather than unilateral measures. The
Fine Gael Party manifesto for the 1987 election stated that FG policy
involved opposition to apartheid including sanctions.[44] In October 1986,
the then Minister for Foreign Affairs, Mr. Peter Barry when speaking at
the Fine Gael Ard Fheis during the debate on foreign affairs stated that
'action at a minimum by the Twelve in concert will be far more effective
than unilateral measures.[45] Since assuming power in 1987, Fianna Fail
favours the traditional policy line on restrictive measures. Mr. Brian
Lenihan, Minister for Foreign Affairs, in reply to Dail questions regarding
coal has said that Ireland supports such a ban by the Twelve but not
unilaterally.[46]

The de facto primacy of the contemporary Executive over the legislature in parliamentary democracies is particularly relevant to the foreign
policy process. It has been argued that legislatures find it difficult to come
to grips with Government proposals and to subject them to lengthy examination and debate.[47] This is particularly true in Ireland given the weak
tradition of parliamentary committees and the absence of a Foreign
Affairs committee. Nonetheless, the Dail does have procedures which
enable it to influence the policy process.

Parliamentary questions are the most readily available mechanism for
getting information from Government and for exercising a degree of
control over ongoing policy. Between 1985-86 there were a total of 185

questions on South Africa; in any one year there are over 2,000 questions in all. Deputies Noel Browne, Ruairi Quinn, Barry Desmond and Proinsias de Rossa asked over 50 percent of the total although forty deputies tabled questions on South Africa. (Appendix L lists deputies who tabled questions on South Africa 1959-86.)

The degree of concern with South Africa rose during the 1980's especially in the last two years. There were 24 questions in 1985 and 16 questions in 1986. This was the result of the deterioration of the situation in South Africa, the Dunnes Stores' strike and discussions of South Africa in EPC. Deputies Tomas MacGiolla, Tony Gregory, Proinsias de Rossa and Gerry Collins were particularly active in scrutinising Government policy. Table 19 lists the number of questions asked by Deputies of each political party from the beginning of the 22nd Dail since 1981 to the end of the 24th Dail in January 1987.

Table 19
Dail Questions on South Africa (1981–1987)

Political Party	No. of Questions	No. of Deputies
Fianna Fail	20	9
Fine Gael	3	3
Labour	6	4
Workers Party	22	2
Other	2	1
TOTAL	53	19

Source: Dail Debates, Vol. 326–368

South Africa is raised from time to time during the debates on the Estimates of the Department of Foreign Affairs. Private Members' Motions have been used on two occasions to raise this issue. In May 1978, Deputy Richie Ryan introduced a motion which condemned apartheid; the reason for introducing it was to publicly acknowledge the UN International Anti-apartheid Year.[48] Only six deputies spoke during the debate which concentrated on the evils of apartheid. A number of deputies did however enlarge the debate to raise the question of Cuban troops in Angola and violations of human rights in other parts of the globe. In March 1981, this device was used again to debate the rugby tour to South Africa. There was considerable disagreement on this occasion. The Labour Party motion suggested that steps should be taken to sever all trade and economic links with South Africa. The Government and the Minister for Foreign Affairs, Mr. Brian Lenihan, given the policy line on unilateral measures, tabled an amendment which emphasised internationally agreed measures.[49] The resolution was not therefore adopted unanimously as the Labour Party refused to accept the amendment.

The Dunnes Stores' strike ensured that the Oireachtas would focus on South Africa. There were many parliamentary questions and the Commitee on Cooperation with Developing Countries decided to examine Apartheid and Development in Southern Africa in 1985 and early 1986. Its report assessed the effects of apartheid on South Africa and in the surrounding region. Attention was paid in the report to the question of sanctions and the attitude of various actors to the use of this instrument. The report concluded that

— there is no doubt about the support of the majority of the black population for sanctions
— that South Africa's neighbouring states also supported sanctions.[50]

Having heard evidence from the Department of Foreign Affairs, the Anti-Apartheid Movement, the Dunnes Stores' strikers, Fruit Importers of Ireland and the non-governmental aid agencies, the Committee recommended that 'a complete ban be imposed on the importation of all South African fruit and vegetables'.[51] It was argued that this would 'have a value beyond its actual economic effect both in terms of encouraging other Governments and of maintaining the morale of those working for peaceful change in South Africa'.[52] This report constituted a further source of pressure on the Government of the time regarding unilateral measures. Although the Oireachtas does not concern itself with foreign affairs to any great extent, South Africa is one of the issues that interests a core of committed deputies and senators. During the Dunnes Stores' strike, a small group of deputies actively canvassed the Government to adopt a unilateral ban.

The Development Cooperation Dimension Ireland, despite its colonial past and a traditional anti-imperialist stance has no great history of development cooperation. A number of factors converged in the early 1970's which led to the establishment of a policy of cooperation with the Third World. First, the UN established an ambitious target for official development aid for the second UN development decade (1970-1980); countries were to aim for a target of 0.7 percent of GNP by 1975 or by 1980 at the latest.[53] Ireland's record was in stark contrast to this target. Second, Ireland joined the EC in 1973 which meant that Ireland's aid performance would be examined by a reference group. Third, the recession induced by the oil crisis brought the entire world economic order into disarray, and discussion of the new international economic order dominated the agenda.

In 1973 the Government decided to increase Ireland's development aid by expanding expenditure through multilateral channels and by establishing a bilateral aid programme. Because total expenditure was likely to remain low in global terms, it was decided to choose a number of priority countries and to concentrate aid in those countries. Four African states were designated as priority areas, Zambia, Tanzania, Lesotho and the Sudan. One of the selection criteria related to special political circumstances. Lesotho was deliberately chosen because of its economic dependence on South Africa. Almost 57 percent of total bilateral aid goes to these four countries. There is therefore a direct link between the wider concerns of Irish foreign policy and development cooperation. (Appendix M provides figures on the flow of Official Development Assistance to the priority countries in the period 1981-1985). Since 1984, Ireland has had direct dealings with the Southern African Development Coordination Conference (SADCC) discussed in Chapter Two. Finance has been granted to a number of projects designed to make the SADCC region more self sufficient in food. A Memorandum of Understanding was signed in 1985 between Ireland and the SADCC country responsible for food security, Zimbabwe. Another project with Swaziland concerns manpower training.[54]

The Committee on Cooperation with Developing Countries clearly established a link between apartheid and the economic condition of its neighbouring states. It concluded in its report on apartheid cited above that

the Committee feels that international support for South Africa's neighbouring countries should be sustained and strengthened. Particular support will be required in the event of the imposition of more stringent sanctions on South Africa.[55]

Therefore there is ample parliamentary support for Ireland's adoption of Lesotho as a priority country and for support to SADCC.

Conclusions

Although Ireland's economic links with South Africa are not sizeable in international terms, material interests are considered when policy is being fashioned. Trade with South Africa has increased despite the fact that there is no official trade promotion. South African investment in Ireland is a sensitive economic issue for any Irish Government. The protection of jobs at Shannon is accorded a high priority.

The Anti-Apartheid Movement together with the development co-operation lobby ensure that Ireland's policy towards South Africa is scrutinised. However, it took the Dunnes Stores' strike to mobilise public opinion. The strike provided those seeking restrictive measures against South Africa with an opportunity to lobby the Government. In response to the strike, the Anti-Apartheid Movement, Trocaire, trades unions, the Irish Commission for Justice and Peace, the Oireachtas Committee on Cooperation with Developing Countries, and a core of active deputies and senators began to lobby the Government and were ultimately successful. The unilateral ban on the importation of fruit and vegetables would not have materialised without the strike.

The story of the unilateral measure shows just how cautious and reactive foreign policy making in Ireland is. Although events in South Africa were deteriorating rapidly from 1984 onwards, Ireland was not going to stray from the traditional policy line on sanctions. The unilateral ban was the result of sustained external pressure on the Government and the sympathy of a number of Ministers on the issue.

■ CHAPTER 5 ■
Conclusions and Policy Recommendations

I reland's policy towards South Africa has been refined over the last 30 years in response to changing circumstances in Southern Africa, internal developments in South Africa, the approach of other countries and activity at the UN and the EEC. During the 1960's, the main thrust of Ireland's policy consisted of condemnations of apartheid at the UN which was regarded as the most appropriate arena for consideration of this issue. The tenor of official statements displayed an abhorrence of racial discrimination, which Mr. Sean Lemass, the Taoiseach, described as being contrary to sound moral principals.[1] A residual sympathy towards South Africa manifested itself. For instance when referring to his condemnation of the Sharpeville massacre in 1960, the Minister for External Affairs, Mr. Frank Aiken, stated that 'Ireland was not actuated by any hostility towards that country and we have always tried to express our views on this problem with moderation'.[2] Ireland did not favour the adoption of punitive measures such as a boycott of South African goods. Indeed, the Government was concerned with Ireland's trade deficit and public agencies continued to have contact with South Africa. South Africa was not a sensitive policy issue at this time.

The policy line began to change towards the end of the 1960's; state agencies were requested to refrain from interaction with South Africa and export promotion ended. This change may be attributed to the tougher line which was being adopted by the UN on apartheid and the role of the Anti-Apartheid Movement in Ireland. Sporting contacts were discouraged and grants were used as a carrot in this regard. Support for limited sanctions especially after the events of Soweto (1976) materialised. Participation in EPC from 1973 onwards offered a further avenue for the articulation of policy towards South Africa. In December 1977, the Minister for Foreign Affairs, Mr. Michael O'Kennedy claimed that within 'the process of political consultation we have been actively promoting a development of economic sanctions against South Africa'[3]

The deteriorating situation in South Africa in 1984 focussed the attention of the international community on this part of the globe. Apartheid was high on the agenda of the UN, the Commonwealth, the Nordic Council and the European Community. All countries including Ireland were forced to review their policies and the kinds of policy instruments they were willing to adopt. In Ireland pressure for change emanated not only from the international environment but also the domestic arena. What began as a localised industrial relations dispute in July 1984 (the Dunnes Stores' Strike) led to an unilateral ban on the importation of South African fruit and vegetables in March 1986.

The Multilateral Dimension

A central theme underlying Ireland's policy towards South Africa is support for multilateral diplomacy. As Ireland does not have diplomatic relations with South Africa, it relies on activity at the UN and in the European Community. Prior to EC membership in 1973, the UN was the major forum for elaborating a policy towards South Africa. Since then, participation in EPC has added another layer to the policy process and additional policy options. Effective multilateral diplomacy requires coalition building with 'likeminded' states to ensure that one's influence is increased and that policy outcomes are congruent with national policies. There is no great tension apparent between Ireland's involvement at the UN on this issue and in EPC. The cleavage which exists among the EC countries on South Africa transfers to the General Assembly of the UN.

The UN Policy at the UN follows the well established principles that have been built up since Ireland joined in 1955. Ireland's voting record and the content of 'EOV's' display considerable consistency which suggests that positions are carefully worked out. Ireland votes in favour of the majority of resolutions on apartheid, uses abstentions to connote disagreement with parts of a resolution and a 'no' vote when there are serious reservations. Participation in EPC has not led Ireland to alter the general trend of its voting behaviour. It is still to the forefront of the industrial countries condemning apartheid at the UN. Asmal's fear expressed in 1979 that Ireland would have to approximate its policies to those of the larger countries has not proved to be well founded.

An important feature of Ireland's activity at the UN is collaboration with 'likeminded' states, notably, Greece, Denmark, Sweden, Austria, Finland, Norway and Iceland. The small West European countries (NATO and Neutral) with some exceptions, have a voting profile which differs greatly from the larger industrial countries. The resolution on 'Concerted international action' is sponsored by these countries and is a bridge-building exercise with the Third World coalition.

Ireland does not support comprehensive UN sanctions against South Africa, nor will it endorse the use of force. On restrictive measures, Ireland supports mandatory sanctions enforced by the Security Council that are binding on all of the Member States. The Irish formula on sanctions is that such measures should be selective, graduated and carefully chosen. Ireland supports the arms embargo, a ban on new investments, and loans, an end to trade promotion, an oil embargo, a prohibition on the sale of krugerrands, an end to nuclear collaboration, and an end to military cooperation including the sale of computers to the South African security forces. Because of the UK/USA veto in the Security Council, Ireland has increasingly looked to EPC as an arena for developing its policy towards South Africa.

The EEC South Africa became an issue on the EPC agenda in 1976 when the first declaration on Southern Africa was made. Given that this is one of the traditional areas of concern for Irish foreign policy, considerable attention was paid by Irish policy-makers to the evolution of the EPC debate. The only policy measure with teeth to emerge in the 1970's was the Code of Conduct which was actively promoted by Great Britain. The Code was favoured by Ireland as an EC measure, but did not apply to any Irish companies. In May 1978, the Code was described as a first step in increasing pressure on South Africa; the Minister for Foreign Affairs, Mr. Michael O'Kennedy, hoped that it would soon be followed by other measures.[4] Since then, no Irish Minister has critically assessed the Code and the manner of its implementation.

Ireland had to wait until 1985 for any real discussion of restrictive measures against South Africa in EPC. The deteriorating situation in South Africa, pressure from the ACP states and discussion in the Commonwealth and the UN forced South Africa to the top of the EPC agenda. The ensuing debate was tortuous and conflict ridden because of the need for consensus, which is difficult to achieve. A deep cleavage, highlighted by UN voting behaviour, exists within EPC on how condemnation of apartheid should be translated into concrete policy action. There are in essence two groups with a number of countries willing to go along with a consensus. The smaller countries, notably, Greece, Denmark, the Netherlands, Spain and Ireland favour EEC sanctions in the fight against apartheid. Denmark, however, is the only member state willing to impose a total ban on trade.

Italy, Belgium and Luxembourg do not exercise a lead function on this issue but have shown a willingness to go along with sanctions. France which at one time adopted a policy stance akin to the other two large states has since 1985 been willing to accept a harder line. Germany, Britain and Portugal, for a variety of reasons, are deeply hostile to the use of sanctions. This latter group because of the need for consensus have managed to delay but ultimately not prevent the adoption of EC restrictive measures.

The September 1985 package, which included a withdrawal of military attaches, an embargo on the importation and exportation of arms, a prohibition on collaboration in the nuclear field, an oil embargo and agreement to discourage cultural, scientific and sporting contacts was a delaying tactic and a political signal to South Africa that the Community might be forced to adopt harsher measures. The 1985 negotiations highlighted the depth of division on this issue among the member states and signalled the difficulties that would emerge in 1986.

The Netherlands on taking over the Presidency of the Council in January 1986 accorded high priority to South Africa. A meeting with the leaders of the frontline states in February of that year and the report of the Commonwealth Eminent Persons Group in June 1986, coupled with renewed repression in South Africa itself forced those countries opposing sanctions to reassess their approach. Sanctions were high on the agenda of the European Council at The Hague in June 1986 and a mini-sanctions package was adopted in September 1986. Britain, Germany, and Portugal were ultimately forced to agree to the measures in the interests of Community solidarity.

Concessions to partners rather than a reappraisal of their approach to sanctions explains this change. Those countries opposing sanctions did get considerable concessions in the bargaining game. First, collective agreement was considerably delayed by the large countries. Second, the agreement excluded coal which was by far the most important item. Third, Community action is considerably weaker than the Scandinavian measures and the US Comprehensive Anti-Apartheid Act of 1986. The exclusion of coal rendered the agreement largely symbolic, reduced the credibility of collective EC action and demonstrated the limits of this form of foreign policy collaboration. It did however breach the stated policies of the UK and Germany who had traditionally opposed sanctions in principle.

Since September 1986, when the sanctions package was agreed, there has been little movement on South Africa in EPC and it is unlikely that the sanctions issue will be reopened in the near future. Policy has reached a plateau and may remain there for some time. Sanctions as a means of effecting change in South Africa are not high on the agenda at the moment. Earlier in 1987 in an attempt to get some movement on South Africa in EPC, the Netherlands suggested that the Community should develop a Code of Principles for post-apartheid South Africa. Agreement was reached on such principles at official level which included a commitment to political unity, protection for minority groups and equality before the law. Sir Geoffrey Howe, the British Foreign Secretary, blocked the adoption and publication of the Code in May 1987. He argued that the Botha Government would not be receptive to a public statement by the EC and that such a move would merely thwart progress in South Africa. The Dutch Foreign Minister, Mr. Hans van der Broek, maintained that a public statement on post-apartheid South Africa would be an essential part of EC strategy which aimed to combine sanctions with confidence-building measures.[5] Disagreement on South Africa among the Member States is as wide as ever.

Ireland and EPC. Irish Foreign Ministers and senior diplomats are committed to EPC as a form of collaboration and place a high premium on forging consensus among the Member States. One of Ireland's most senior diplomats describes the benefits of EPC in the following terms:

> The Irish experience in EPC, (in my view,) has been very positive. Irish foreign policy now concerns itself with a greater range and depth of issues systematically and regularly within a context where its own approach and views are combined with and help shape the collective response of the Community as a whole and of the Twelve. The result has been an increase and extension of our ability to exercise influence on the international stage since it seems to me to be self evident that small countries will increase their influence when acting in combination with others rather than alone.[6]

EPC has become an important pillar of Irish foreign policy[7] and Irish foreign policy makers have not been faced with irreconcilable conflicts of interest to date.[8]

Has EPC acted as a constraint on Ireland or has it been a means for increased influence on this issue? During the 1987 referendum on the Single European Act (SEA), those opposing ratification argued that Ireland had watered down its position on key international issues, including apartheid, in order to keep in line with the other EC countries.[9] The evidence of this study on UN voting and on participation in EPC does not support this conclusion. Given the difficulty of getting mandatory sanctions at UN level, concerted action by the Twelve is seen as a means of developing policy options. This is not to argue that the requirement for consensus does not inhibit action against South Africa. Failure to agree to a ban on coal in September 1986 meant that Ireland did not ban the importation of South African coal, a measure it was willing to adopt provided agreement was reached at EC level. On the other hand, Germany and Britain would never have agreed to sanctions without pressure from the other Community countries.

As one of the Member States favouring concerted EC action against South Africa, Irish Ministers have regarded each Community measure as a step towards increasing pressure and not as an end in itself. The Code of Conduct was described as a first step and the 1985 package as a minimum.[10] The then Taoiseach, Dr. Garret FitzGerald, described the outcome of the Hague Summit in June 1986 as a second best solution and a modest step forward.[11] In October 1986, Mr. Peter Barry, the Minister for Foreign Affairs, argued that Ireland would have wished the Community to go further and that it would continue to work towards further common measures by the Twelve.[12] To date EPC agreement has fallen short of Ireland's stated policy. Put simply, Ireland has been one of those countries in EPC attempting to enlarge the scope of EC policies on this issue. Collaboration with countries such as Denmark and the Netherlands has been a feature of this endeavour. Given the confidential nature of the EPC process, it is not possible to assess the contribution of any one country to the process.

Unilateral Measures

The delay during 1985/1986 on the imposition of collective measures caused considerable difficulty at domestic level in Ireland because of the stark contrast between the action of a small group of Dunnes Stores' workers in refusing to handle South African goods and prevarication at European Community level. The strike was a daily symbol of the willingness of a small group of Irish workers to sacrifice their jobs on an issue far from Irish shores. It provided the Anti-Apartheid Movement with a powerful catalyst and extensive media attention. Gradually, the Irish Congress of Trade Unions, Trocaire, the Irish Commission for Justice and Peace and the Oireachtas Committee on Cooperation with Developing Countries called for concrete action. The demand for unilateral measures was met with the well established policy line which favoured concerted global and regional measures.

The imposition of a ban on the importation of fruit and vegetables in March 1986 was a decision taken against the considered policy line of the last 20 years and against official advice to Cabinet. Considerable conflict was engendered at official level and in Cabinet about the decision. It would appear as if the Department of Foreign Affairs remained steadfast in its reservations concerning unilateral measures up to the Cabinet decision of December 1985. Replies by the Minister for Foreign Affairs to Dail questions in the latter half of 1985 display no change in the official line.

The decision to adopt a unilateral ban was at no time an active and calculated response to changing circumstances in South Africa. It was a response to intense domestic pressure which in itself would not have been sufficient without the support of a number of Ministers in Cabinet. The Minister for Labour, Deputy Ruairi Quinn, was largely instrumental in getting the issue to Cabinet and the Taoiseach Dr. Garret FitzGerald played an important role in keeping the issue on the agenda once it had got there. There appears to have been little consideration of the symbolic value of unilateral measures and the leverage that such measures might bestow at UN and EC level. The Anti-Apartheid Movement in evidence to the Oireachtas Committee on Cooperation with Developing Countries argued that Irish policy had not adapted to the new situation in South Africa.[13] This analysis of how the ban on fruit and agricultural products emerged supports this conclusion. There were tactical reasons for opting for unilateral measures at that stage given the state of flux on policy. As the EC tried to edge its way towards a sanctions package, Ireland did in fact gain leverage from the unilateral ban.

Since then the traditional policy line has reasserted itself. In October 1986, Mr. Peter Barry, the Minister for Foreign Affairs, stated in the Dail that 'we had hoped that by taking that unilateral action it would be an example to other countries to follow as far as we went. This was not so. Nobody else followed us, therefore, that points to the fact that unilateral action perhaps is not the wisest course'.[14] Replies to a series of Dail questions in 1987 suggest that although the present Government will not dismantle the existing unilateral measure because it commanded wide support from all quarters of the house, there is little prospect under foreseeable circumstances of further unilateral measures.[15] The Minister for Foreign Affairs, Mr. Brian Lenihan, said in reply to a Dail question on coal that the Government had no plans to introduce a unilateral ban but still favoured a Community ban.[16] This statement was accompanied by a reiteration of the belief that concerted action is far more effective than any unilateral measure that Ireland might take. Thus the old policy line is reasserting itself and future action is bound up with developments in the European Community and the United Nations.

The Scandinavian countries Since 1946 Ireland's policy stance began to diverge from that of a number of countries which had been 'likeminded' on South Africa. Traditionally, the Scandinavian states favoured mandatory action by the UN Security Council. By October 1985, in a communique outlining the *Nordic Programme for Action Against South Africa*, it is argued that 'in view of the unique character of the Apartheid regime, lack of agreement in the UN Security Council on mandatory sanctions against South Africa should not prevent individual countries taking measures of their own'.[17] In 1986, Norway and Denmark opted for a complete ban on imports from and exports to South Africa followed by Sweden in 1987. Denmark did not feel bound by EPC although it is not yet clear if it will be able to prevent South African goods from reaching its market via other EC states. Participation in the customs union clearly impairs the effectiveness of unilateral trade measures by any Community country.

Economic interests versus ethical concerns Policy towards South Africa is moulded by the tension between direct economic interests and a moral concern with the evils of apartheid. It has been argued that because of the narrow range of direct national interests at stake, Ireland finds itself at the 'moralist' rather than *'real politic'* end of the EPC spectrum on issues such as South Africa.[18] Careful examination of Ireland's approach suggests that Ireland is loath to pursue policy options which may impinge on material interests. Senator Catherine Bulbulia, when listing the options Ireland supports at the UN and in the EEC, made the point that Ireland has little direct interest in these areas. She suggests that 'it is a painless and high minded exercise to say we support these types of mandatory sanctions. The proposed areas of which we are involved are the importation of fruit and vegetables, timber, clothing, furniture and wool and the export of computers, electronic materials and the large investments of De Beers in the Shannon Free Area'.[19] South African investment in Ireland was a sensitive issue during the debate on unilateral measures because of the importance of De Beers and Boart Hardmetals to Shannon.

105

The desire to protect South Africa as an export market was also apparent. These economic considerations, particularly investment, will surface again in any debate on restrictive measures.

The protection of almost 1,000 jobs in Shannon will always be accorded high priority by an Irish Government. Do these jobs necessarily have to inhibit the adoption of restrictive measures? If Ireland imposed a trade embargo could this deny the Shannon companies necessary raw materials? At present most of the raw material for the De Beers plant comes from Zaire although the Shannon plant is also used as a clearing house for industrial diamonds manufactured in South Africa itself. Would De Beers or the South African Government use this investment to retaliate against any Irish action? Is it likely that the companies would decide to withdraw from Shannon unilaterally given that they are there a long time, have a pool of highly trained workers and are located in a tax free zone with a high return on capital employed? If it is unlikely then the question is whether or not the companies would respond to pressure from the South African authorities. It is noteworthy that a section of the South African business community has taken the initiative to meet with the ANC to discuss post-apartheid South Africa. The perceptions and interests of the South African Government and the business community are not necessarily congruent. Although South African investment in Ireland is politically sensitive, fears about the viability of the Shannon companies are not necessarily well founded.

Foreign policy making We concluded in Chapter Four that foreign policy making on South Africa has been cautious and reactive since the recent wave of unrest. This contrasts with the Scandinavian countries whose foreign policies have strong political direction and are the product of debate in well formed 'foreign policy communities', including parliamentary committees, Institutes for International Affairs, the universities and specialist journals. The Irish 'foreign policy community' remains a 'shadowy source of influence'.[20] Yet South Africa is an issue with an 'attentive public' in Ireland. The Anti-Apartheid Movement has ensured that Government policy is scrutinised. South Africa as a foreign policy issue does not receive sustained political attention. A large number of Irish politicians are generally sympathetic towards the aspirations of the Anti-Apartheid Movement but this does not translate into policy initiatives. The road to the unilateral measures demonstrates clearly that if political attention is paid to the issue, official policy will change. In the absence of sustained political direction, policy will be governed by continuity and precedent. Aberach in a study of the relationship between politicians and bureaucrats concludes that the latter bring prudence, moderation and the avoidance of risk to bear on any policy issue. Policy change of any fundamental kind requires political direction.[21]

Future policy options South Africa is a country in a state of acute crisis.

Despite widespread and deep rooted internal opposition to the system, the South African authorities refuse to bend. Mr. Brian Lenihan, the Minister for Foreign Affairs, said at the UN General Assembly in September 1987 that

> the events of the last year have brought no comfort to those who hope to see the Apartheid System dismantled and the emergence in South Africa of multi-racial democracy in its stead ... The Government in South Africa continues to defy international opinion and has yet to demonstrate clearly that it is prepared to engage in genuine reform and to commence meaningful political dialogue with the authentic leaders of the majority community.[22]

Yet the demands of the black and coloured population for full democratic and economic rights and a political system based on 'one man one vote' will not go away. The South African Government may succeed in restoring a measure of calm by imposing yet more draconian laws but for how long? There was a long period of muted opposition between Sharpeville (1960) and Soweto (1976) but a very short time span between Soweto and the present wave of unrest. The question facing the industrialised countries including Ireland is what measures they should adopt in order to pressurise the South African authorities to negotiate change with the black population in order to prevent the present unrest from descending into a sustained and bloody civil war.

Policy Recommendations

The path from policy description to prescription is not an easy one in relation to South Africa. Successive Irish Governments have been committed to 'doing something' about South Africa including the imposition of selective economic sanctions. What should Ireland now contemplate in addition to existing measures within the terms of the formula favouring graduated selective sanctions? What does Ireland do if as is claimed by Orkin that 'nearly all of the major powers are still "talking shop" with South Africa'?[23] And in South Africa itself the Botha Government is stronger than it has been since the present wave of unrest was unleashed in 1984. Austin (1986), when attempting to establish a framework for UK policy towards South Africa, uses an apposite quote from Burke which reads:

> The use of force is but temporary. It may subdue for a moment, but it does not remove the necessity of subduing again, and a nation is not governed which is perpetually to be conquered.[24]

As Austin states the question about South Africa for policy makers in search of policy is, how long is temporary?[25]

In Chapter One, a series of policy options were outlined including dip-

Table 20

Table 20
Summary of Ireland's measures against South Africa
(adapted from Hanlon and Omond (1987) pp.300-2)

Measure		Unilateral	EC	UN
1.	Total Embargo	—	—	—
2.	Ban on Sales and Technology Transfer			
2.1	Ban on exports to South Africa	—	—	—
2.2	Arms	—	Military attaches Arms embargo	SC418 (1977)
2.3	Oil	—	Oil embargo	
2.4	Nuclear	—	New collaboration	SC569 (1985)
2.5	Computers	—	Ban for security forces	SC569 (1985)
2.6	Other	—	—	—
2.7	Services	—	—	—
2.8	Export Promotion	1970	—	SC569 (1985)
2.9	Regulation of Trade	—	—	—
3	Ban on Purchases	—	—	—
3.1	Total Ban on Imports	—	—	—
3.2	Agricultural Products	fruit and vegetables	—	—
3.3	Minerals and Steel	favours EC ban on coal	iron & steel	—
3.4	Precious Metals Diamonds & gold coins	—	Krugerrands	—
3.5	Purchase of arms	—	ban	SC558 (1984)
3.6	Other	—	—	—
4.	Financial Ban	—	—	—
4.1	Total Investment ban	—	—	—
4.2	New Investments	—	ban	SC569 (1985)
4.3	Total Loan Ban	—	—	—
4.4	Some Loans	Voluntary ban	—	—
4.5	Prevent IMF Loans	Did not favour 1982 loan	—	—

SC 418 (1977)-Mandatory   SC 569 (1985)-Voluntary
SC 558 (1984)-Voluntary

lomatic measures, a cultural, sports and an academic boycott and sanctions. Table 20 provides a summary of the measures Ireland has adopted to date.

For the future Ireland should take action in the following areas.

Diplomatic measures Ireland should continue to use diplomatic channels and international organisations to make its views on South Africa known, to exhort the South African Government to begin negotiations, and to continue pressing for human rights in South Africa. It should maintain contact with opposition forces in South Africa. Successive Irish Governments have been willing to meet with representatives of the ANC. Ireland should not support Chief Buthelezi because although he remains formally opposed to the 'homelands' policy, he has developed links with the 'homelands' Governments and supports ethnic division.[26] His position on sanctions has endeared him to the UK and the Federal Republic of Germany.

A visa regime for South African visitors should be introduced notwithstanding the difficulties outlined in Chapter Four. Ireland is one of the few European Community countries not imposing such a requirement. It is a policy measure which would not affect Ireland's economic interests nor does it impose a burden on South Africa's black popularion. A visa regime would enable the Government to refuse entry to South African citizens for conferences and sporting events which would strengthen the implementation of the sports, cultural, and academic boycott. Visa requirements could well prove important in ensuring that Ireland would not be used for sanctions busting by South African citizens.

The Government, having reviewed this measure, decided that a visa regime would pose difficulty for Irish aid workers and the aid programme in Lesotho. This argument although it has some validity should not prevent a policy option being adopted which would send a direct signal to the white population. In any case the Government should direct Irish aid workers to minimise their contact with South Africa.

Development cooperation and positive measures EC policy towards South Africa is two-dimensional, with positive and restrictive measures. The positive measures outlined in Chapter Three are an important component of the overall policy because they are designed to aid the victims of apartheid. They should not be the only policy because on their own they will not change the fundamentals of the apartheid system.

Aid to SADCC as a regional organisation should be increased because it provides the only long term strategy whereby the countries adjacent to South Africa might achieve a degree of economic viability and independdence. At EC level Ireland should press for increased aid to SADCC and should be mindful lest those countries hostile to restrictive measures (UK and Germany), use aid as a trade-off in return for less pressure on sanctions. This appears to have happened at the Commonwealth Summit (October 1987) where the British Prime Minister succeeded in preventing further sanctions but took the lead on support for Mozambique and the reconstruction of the Limpopo railway.[27] Goodison in an analysis of

European aid to the SADCC countries concluded that when the SADCC required immediate support to try to insulate itself from the developing crisis in South Africa, the British and German Governments decreased their aid (1980/1985). When the demand was for restrictive action (1985-1986) these two countries began to increase their aid to SADCC again. Goodison claims that the principal aim of this policy is to give the impression of distancing the EC from South Africa, without giving anything materially in its relationship with South Africa.[28] In the event of stringent sanctions, the industrialised countries must step up aid to the frontline states to ensure that the adverse effects of sanctions are minimised.

The Irish Anti-Apartheid Movement for many years requested that Ireland give direct aid to the ANC and SWAPO: a number of other European countries, notably, Sweden, Norway, Denmark, the Netherlands, Italy and Spain do so.[29] The Oireachtas Committee endorsed this call in a later report.[30] Official reticence concerning direct aid to the ANC and SWAPO derives from the question of armed struggle which Ireland will not endorse. Humanitarian aid to the victims of apartheid including refugees could be stepped up and channelled through a fund for the victims of apartheid as part of the bilateral aid programme. This recommendation is made despite the fact that the Official Development Assistance (ODA) budget has been cut by £11m (26%) for 1988.[31]

The parliamentary dimension A small number of deputies and senators ask all of the parliamentary questions on this issue and Irish MEPs are not active on South Africa in the European Parliament. Many of them fail to register a vote on the major EP resolutions and during 1986 a number of those who did failed to support a special budgetary line on aid to the SADCC states (November 1986). The absence of an Oireachtas Committee on Foreign Affairs has limited parliamentary scrutiny of Ireland's policy. Irish parliamentarians, (Oireachtas and European Parliament) could become more active in the Association of West European Parliamentarians for Action Against Apartheid (AWEPAA) which plays an important role in informing parliamentarians about South Africa and of the policy positions of various countries. It has become a significant lobbying group in the European Parliament and in a number of European countries. A small number of politicians attend the meetings at present. An Oireachtas Committee on Foreign Affairs would contribute to a widening of the debate on foreign policy as senior diplomats would have to make submissions to such a committee and would have to explain how and why foreign policy decisions were arrived at. It would provide an opportunity for other points of view to emerge so that a wider range of policy options could be assessed.

Moral Suasion Government cannot interfere with the freedom of citizens to travel abroad be they sports people, entertainers or those wishing to take up jobs in South Africa. It can, however, strive to create a moral climate which discourages such action. Development education has a role to play in raising awareness about issues such as apartheid. Government support for information campaigns on South Africa contributes to an informed public opinion. Furthermore, the Government should from time to time inform organisations representing sports people, musicians, entertainers etc as well as employment agencies or firms who recruit for South Africa of its policy on apartheid.

Sanctions The sanctions movement is muted at present in the Commonwealth and the European Community. The Canadian Foreign Minister spoke of 'sanctions fatigue' at the Commonwealth Summit in Vancouver (October 1987).[32] If however the situation inside South Africa deteriorates even further, the debate will return to sanctions. It is argued in Chapter One that sanctions are an important corollary of internal opposition because South Africa has been relatively immune to diplomatic initiatives. Sanctions have the potential to reduce the capacity of the South African Government to suppress the majority population and to impose a tax on apartheid by steadily increasing the cost of maintaining the system. This can be achieved by denying South Africa essential goods and by hitting at the morale of the white population. Sanctions will not, however, achieve an immediate transformation, rather they will contribute to a steady build-up of pressure which may lead to negotiations. The Co-Chairman of the Eminent Persons Group concluded that a greater descent into violence is inevitable in South Africa unless the major western states that have trade weight with South Africa really bring pressure to bear.[33]

The experience of the last year (1987) underlines the fact that partial sanctions will not bring apartheid tumbling down. *The Economist* in an assessment of all restrictive measures concluded that they had affected only about eight percent of South Africa's exports. The decline in the price of oil cut South Africa's import bill while the price of gold (largest foreign currency earner) soared, thus strengthening the South African economy. Restrictions on the export of coal have had some impact. Coal exports amounted to 9.8 million tons in the first quarter of 1987 in contrast to 11.4 million tons in 1986. The planned expansion of a terminal for coal exports was delayed.[34] The South African Government has ceased to publish monthly production figures of minerals in an attempt to cover up the down turn in the production of coal.[35] By July 1987 EC imports of iron and steel still stood at two-thirds the monthly average before the September 1986 ban.[36] Companies were continuing to import steel under long-term contracts. The European Parliament in a report concludes that it is impossible to determine if the contracts had been backdated.[37] The spirit if not the letter of Ireland's unilateral ban may have been breached by Swaziland, South Africa and Irish importers.

Disinvestment by foreign companies has gathered momentum. In 1986/1987 over 78 US companies including IBM, General Motors and Exxon have left South Africa. In addition, the British bank, Barclays has succumbed to pressure from the British Anti-Apartheid Movement and sold off its holdings in South Africa. In some cases, the withdrawal amounted only to a change of ownership; many departing companies continue to supply components and technology.[38] Nonetheless, disinvestment has contributed to a decline in business confidence. Since the loan crisis in August 1985, South Africa's credit rating has remained low. One writer argues that 'South Africa is in the process of entering the state of a very costly "siege economy" — a state from which it can actually only emerge a loser'.[39]

An important issue in relation to sanctions is consideration of the most appropriate arena for the imposition of restrictive measures. Ireland's stated policy of favouring mandatory UN sanctions is undoubtedly the option with the greatest promise of effectiveness. Mandatory UN sanctions are the preferred policy of all countries favouring restrictive measures because it reduces the possibility of sanctions busting and is equitable for all member states concerned. Concerted action would send the strongest signal to South Africa, would increase its isolation and would undermine the morale of the white population. The veto power of the US and Britain in the Security Council makes selective mandatory sanctions, let alone comprehensive ones, difficult to achieve for the foreseeable future. Nonetheless, Ireland should continue to work with the other smaller European countries at the UN to form a bridge with 'likeminded' African states in an effort to promote concerted international action. The yearly resolution on concerted international action for the elimination of apartheid may well be reviewed because of policy changes apparent in Scandinavian states. These countries may press for additional measures which Ireland may or may not support.

Ireland is very committed to collective EPC measures on South Africa — from the mid 1970's onwards EPC was cited again and again as an arena for pursuing an anti-apartheid policy. Yet the mini-sanctions package which was the result of long and tortuous negotiations is largely symbolic and much less severe than the later US package. The South African government has powerful allies in Britain and Germany because of the extent of their material interests in the region and their hardline policies towards restrictive measures. During the domestic debate in Ireland on unilateral measures there was extensive discussion of likely developments in EPC. The Minister for Foreign Affairs, Mr. Peter Barry, reiterated time and time again that the EEC was moving to collective action and that Ireland should await the outcome of these deliberations before engaging in unilateral measures.

What strategies should Ireland now pursue given the experience of the 1985 and 1986 negotiations? Irish policy makers together with their counterparts in other Community countries who accord a high priority to apartheid need to review policy and to establish the framework for long term measures. There is a need to ensure that South Africa does not become an issue of low priority, — the Belgian Presidency of the Council (January 1987 to June 1987) devoted minimal public attention to apartheid. The proposed charter of principles on post-apartheid South Africa would complement the sanctions package and would establish guidelines for EC policy, somewhat like the Venice Declaration on the Middle East. The fact that Britain blocked the publication of the principles shows the extent to which it is prepared to paralyse EC agreement.

The sanctions movement is much more muted at present than it has been over the last two years. It is as if the passage of the US, EC, Scandinavian, and Commonwealth measures signalled the end of a particular wave of interest. With 'likeminded' countries in the Community Ireland should try to get agreement on coal as this would at least implement the entire Hague package and would give the measures some teeth. The Association of West European Parliamentarians for Action against Apartheid (AWEPAA) has made a joint EC ban its first priority.[40]

Ireland should ensure that certain weaknesses in the 1986 agreement are not repeated. The package contained no provision for an investigations unit or a monitoring body. The measures were implemented in varying ways by a combination of EC law and national directives. The ban on iron and steel was implemented by ECSC law while the ban on new investments was left to the Member States. In Ireland the latter is enforced by the Central Bank's supervision of direct funding abroad, whereas the Belgian authorities issued a letter to the main employer organisations. Germany has not issued any written directive; there is merely a gentlemen's agreement with the main trading and business organisations.[41] The EP report highlights two major loopholes in the oil embargo. First, oil from third world countries stored in bonded warehouses can be delivered to South Africa in transit. Second, the ban does not cover petroleum products. A European Parliament Resolution (30 October 1987) called on the Council to 'draw conclusions from the inadequate way that the decisions taken in EPC have so far been carried out and that suitable Community instruments must now be devised if the Community's credibility is to be preserved.'[42]

The 1986 package did not include Namibia although South Africa continues to occupy that territory. Parallel measures should be imposed on trade with Namibia. This exclusion may provide a facility for circumventing the restrictive measures. The agreement was open-ended. Sanctions will only prove effective if South Africa is made aware of a long term commitment on the part of the Community. Put simply, a progressive timetable detailing the measures that will be adopted if there is no change in South Africa would be much more effective than a once-off set of measures.

Given that Britain and Germany are unlikely to alter their opposition to sanctions in the short term does this mean that the Community policy on South Africa is paralysed? Although all of the member states including Ireland are attached to the principle of consensus, its absence in the past has not prevented a restricted grouping of countries from acting in concert.

During the Falklands war in 1982, the Community acting under Article 113 (Rome Treaty) imposed sanctions against Argentina for one month. During that month, Ireland's policy changed following the outbreak of hostilities — the Government announced that sanctions were no longer appropriate. At a meeting of EEC Foreign Ministers (17 May 1982) Ireland and Italy refused to continue with sanctions but agreed not to allow their countries to be used to permit goods imported from Argentina to enter the territory of other member states. The remaining countries continued to impose sanctions.[43]

Partial agreement may be the only way of developing EC policy at this stage. This strategy was discounted by Ireland in September 1986 because it was felt that a divided Community would send the wrong kind of signal to Pretoria. Yet the South African authorities are well aware of the extent of disagreement in the Community. If those countries supportive of a ban on coal had in fact initiated a partial ban using parallel national measures they would have demonstrated to South Africa that a core of EC states were committed to the Hague package and would have caused acute embarrassment to the three countries unwilling to agree. The difficulty would have been to assemble support from the significant number of countries. France, Italy, Luxembourg and Belgium may not have agreed to partial measures. Nonetheless it is a strategy that deserves consideration when the question of sanctions is raised again. Partial measures could involve non-EEC 'likeminded' countries.

The absence of movement at UN and EC levels may prove to be an alibi for inaction. Ireland retains the freedom to opt for unilateral measures akin to the ban on importation of fruit and vegetables. Unilateral measures have a role in boosting the sanctions movement and in creating a cumulative build-up of pressure. They may act as a powerful symbol at regional level and may pressurise other states into action. This is the approach now adopted by the Scandinavian states; any course of action, however small, supports the opposition movement in South Africa itself.[44] On the other hand, unilateral measures if adopted by a small state are undoubtedly less effective than concerted action. Ireland is a member of a customs union which governs trade with third countries. The free circulation of goods within the market makes it difficult to prevent produce from South Africa entering the Irish market via another Community country. This constraint however has not prevented Denmark from imposing a total ban on trade.

The figures supplied in Chapter Four regarding Swazi exports of citrus fruit to Ireland suggest that a level of sanctions-busting may be occurring. The Irish Government should make a formal request to the Swazi Government to investigate the matter to ensure that the spirit of Irish public policy is not being breached. Ireland has provided official development assistance to Swaziland[45] under the bilateral aid programme and as such Swaziland should respect Irish law and should not aid South Africa to get around Ireland's trade ban. The Government should also approach the

Irish importers if they are using 'back door' methods to import South African fruit and vegetables into Ireland.

Although Ireland ceased to provide public monies for the promotion of trade with South Africa, trade has increased over the last decade. As a prelude to further restrictive measures and in order to establish a data base of information concerning trade with South Africa a licensing system for imports and exports could be put in place. This would ensure that the Government has comprehensive information concerning Ireland's trade with South Africa. If at any time, a decision is taken to further restrict trade, licences could simply be refused for any product. Finland and Sweden require that all imports from South Africa have a special licence and lists of licences are published.[46]

Notwithstanding reservations concerning unilateral measures highlighted above there are two areas that deserve careful consideration — coal and high technology goods. A unilateral ban on coal would help promote the sanctions movement in the European Community. South African coal constitutes such a small proportion of Ireland's imports of this product that alternative supplies could be found. Computers are the most sensitive item exported to South Africa by this country. Ireland's sale of computers has increased in value each year for the last seven years and constituted 27 percent of total exports to South Africa in 1986. South Africa is heavily dependent on imports of high technology goods for its manufacturing sector. Becker makes a cogent argument for restrictions on these products in the following terms:

> Proscription of OECD exports of key high technology intermediate goods to South Africa ... is a real threat, especially to the non-agricultural component of the modern economy. Such a ban would be particularly effective if it were combined with investment restrictions that limit South Africa's ability to engage in the production of import substitutes.[47]

The main advantage of restrictions of this kind is that they would affect the affluent white community rather than the black population. Restrictions on high technology goods would strengthen the implementation of the arms embargo. It is impossible at present to ensure that the South African security forces do not in fact get high technology goods destined for another source. At a minimum, the COCOM list which governs the export of arms, paramilitary and sensitive products to Eastern Europe should be used.[48]

Reflections

Policy towards South Africa appears to have reached a plateau. Leading powers in the industrialised world have successfully managed to stem the sanctions tide. The British Prime Minister, Mrs. Thatcher, has ensured that her preferred policy line of 'no sanctions' has prevented the adoption of further measures by the Commonwealth. Together with Chancellor Kohl, she has prevented the emergence of a consensus in EPC on further measures. In the United States, the Reagan Administration has not been prepared to propose further restrictive measures.[49] The present Irish Government will not implement additional sanctions in the absence of international agreement, agreement that is singularly absent.[50] Yet Governments change and domestic lobbies have made Governments move from established policy. The US Congress prepared to impose further sanctions and will take a lead on this issue.[51] The Dunnes Stores Strike altered Government policy in Ireland.

The sanctions issue will come to the fore again when conditions in South Africa deteriorate further. Then Ireland will have to confront the issue of economic interdependence again, especially South African involvement in Ireland. Although South African involvement in Shannon has not featured prominently in the public debate it has impinged on Government action. A review of this dimension of economic interaction should be undertaken by the Government now to clarify the issues at stake.

The Botha Government may have succeeded in restoring a measure of control, but for how long? South Africa is an inherently unstable society which depends on awesome repression. Given the history of South Africa since 1948 and the experiences of the last four years, it is unlikely that peaceful accommodation is possible between the white minority and the rest of the population. Consequently the international community may have to deal with a situation of increasing violence and repression. In an article entitled 'South Africa: The Revolution Once More Postponed', van der Ropp points out that

> Notwithstanding the failures of the revolutionaries and the corresponding successes of the Government, the latter has not succeeded in retaining the 'status quo ante'. The situation that has arisen can best be described as an 'equilibrium of violence'. Though new unrest can flare up any day, the authorities will long be in a position to quell it. But they would have to resort to increasingly tougher and hence more damaging methods in terms of foreign relations. A look at the schools shows the magnitude of the revolutionary potential there.[52]

Public opinion in the industrial countries may well force Governments to review their policies and to adopt extensive restrictive measures against South Africa. Change in South Africa is a long term process — the political system based on white supremacy will not survive.

Many words have been written and uttered about South Africa; I leave the last word of this study to a black mineworker:

But all my people, and myself
Are black, and being black, have nothing,
Above the pit the grass is green,
As bright and fresh as clear blue skies;
We gaze, and cry out 'Woe' but cries
Of 'Woe' and 'Woe' remain unanswered.[53]

                    B.W. Vilakazi

References

Chapter One: The Issues in Focus

1 Issues before the 40th General Assembly of the UN 1985, pp.27-30
2 *Africa South of the Sahara* 1986, p.64
3 US Department of State, *A Policy Towards South Africa* 1987, p.25
4 *The Observer* 27 September 1987, p.53
5 US Department of State, *A US Policy Towards South Africa* 1987, p.33
6 See Fraser and Obasanjo 1986, pp.156-62 for their views on the process
7 Ibid. p.155
8 Quoted in Hanlon and Omond 1987, p.120
9 Ibid. p.191
10 Ibid. pp.300-65 for a comprehensive analysis of existing sanctions
11 Ibid.
12 Braun and Weiland 1987, pp.7-8
13 Ibid. pp.11-12
14 Hanlon and Omond 1987, pp.141-60, 175-85
15 Quoted in Becker 1986, p.148
16 Margaret Thatcher, press conference 5 August 1986
17 Moorsom 1986, p.87
18 Hanlon and Omond 1987, p.193
19 Ibid., p.222
20 Ibid. pp.222-7
21 Eminent Persons Group, in *Mission to South Africa*, 1986, p.140
22 Trocaire/Irish Commission for Justice and Peace Joint Statement, *Ireland and Sanctions against South Africa*, 29 October 1985
23 Hanlon and Omond 1987, p.193
24 Ibid. p.32
25 Ibid. pp.45-9
26 Orkin 1986, p.13
27 Ibid. p.15
28 Hanlon and Omond 1987, p.210
29 Moorsom 1986, Hanlon and Omond 1987
30 Dail Debates 367:776, 30 May 1986
31 Wolfers 1962, p.71
32 For a discussion of these goals see Keatinge 1978, pp.170-90
33 Dail Debates 265:750, 9 May 1973
34 EOV, 11 December 1984, UN General Assembly
35 Ibid.
36 Dail Debates 178:29, 18 November 1959
37 Keatinge 1973 p.15
38 Amstrup 1976
39 Wallace 1971 p.44
40 Press releases, Catholic Press and Information Office, Dublin
41 Trocaire, Development Cooperation Programme 1986 p.11
42 Macridis 1968 p.9

Chapter Two: Ireland's Stance on South Africa at the United Nations

1 Cited in Holsti 1972, p.422
2 UN *Yearbook 1981*, Chap. VII, p.1495, Article 41, UN Charter
3 *Dail Debates* 286:1538, 11 December 1975
4 Issues before the 40th General Assembly, 1985, p.25
5 Ibid. p.25

6 *Dail Debates* 368:2333, 3 July 1986
7 Keatinge 1978, p.188
8 Keatinge 1973, p.32
9 Cruise O'Brien 1969, p.128; Keatinge 1978, p.76
10 Keatinge 1978, p.75
11 *Dail Debates* 286:498, 27 November 1975
12 Peterson 1986, p.92
13 Dolman 1979, p.57-9
14 *Dail Debates* 286:498, 27 November 1975
15 Proceedings of the General Assembly 1980-86
16 Keatinge 1973, p.284
17 Asmal 1979, p.9
18 General Assembly Resolution 41/35H, 10 November 1986
19 EOV, 7 November 1986, p.4
20 General Assembly Resolution 35/206Q, 16 December 1980
21 *Dail Debates* 294:634, 24 November 1976
22 General Assembly Resolution 41/35H, 10 November 1986
23 Proceedings of the UN General Assembly 1986
24 General Assembly Resolution 35/206C, 16 December 1980
25 EOV, 16 December 1981
26 General Assembly Resolution 36/172D, 17 December 1981
27 General Assembly Resolutions 37/69C, 9 December 1982 and 18/39D, 5 December 1983
28 EOV, 10 December 1985
29 EOV, 20 November 1987, p.3
30 EOV, 11 December 1984
31 General Assembly Resolution 36/172E, 17 December 1981
32 EOV, 5 December 1983
33 General Assembly Resolution 41/35A, 10 November 1986
34 EOV, 7 November 1986
35 EOV, 10 December 1985
36 EOV, 16 December 1981
37 General Assembly Resolution 36/172I, 17 December 1981
38 General Assembly Resolution 32/172L, 17 December 1981
39 General Assembly Resolution 41/35H, 10 November 1986
40 EOV, 11 December 1984 p.4
41 *Dail Debates* 275:922, 5 November 1974
42 *Dail Debates* 265:750, 3 May 1973
43 *Dail Debates* 268:202, November 1973
44 *Dail Debates* 338:833, 3 November 1982
45 Hurwitz 1976
46 Proceedings of the General Assembly, 40th session 1985, p.56
47 *Dail Debates* 307:134, 30 May 1978
48 Hanlon and Omond 1987, p.306
49 Ibid. p.324
50 Ibid. p.196
51 *Dail Debates* 286:502, 27 November 1975

Chapter Three: The European Community, Ireland and South Africa

1 Moorsom 1986, pp.24-6
2 "Sanctions and the South African Economy": Briefing Paper, December 1986, p.2, Overseas Development Institute, London
3 Unpublished EC Commission Staff Paper, 7 October 1987
4 Moorsom 1986, p.83, Hanlon and Omond 1987, pp.250-55
5 Hanlon and Omond 1987, p.255
6 Scott Hopkins Report 1982, Rogers and Bolton 1981
7 Hanlon and Omond 1987, Moorsom 1986
8 Maull 1986, pp.619-26
9 "Sanctions and the South African Economy": Briefing Paper, December 1986, p.1, Overseas Development Institute, London
10 US Department of State, *A US Policy Towards South Africa*, Report of the Secretary of State's Advisory Committee on South Africa, 29 January 1987, p.28

11 EC Communique, Hague Summit, point 15
12 Forde 1987, p.214
13 J. Henchy, *The Irish Times*, Special Supplement, 6 May 1987, p.3
14 J. Finlay, *The Irish Times*, Special Supplement, 6 May 1987, p.2
15 MacKernan 1984, p.22
16 van Praag 1982, p.130
17 Address to the UN General Assembly by Mr Gaston Thorn, in Developments in the European Communities, January 1981, Pr 1 1982, p.117
18 Communique, Meeting of the Foreign Ministers of the frontline states and those of the Community, 4 February 1986, point 5/6
19 Conference of Foreign Ministers, Statement on South Africa, 22 July 1985
20 _____, 4 February 1986, point 6
21 _____, 1 July 1985
22 European Parliament Doc. 1-657/82, 1982 1 July
23 Holland 1985, (B) p.410
24 European Parliament Doc. A 2-58, 86, 10 July 1986, EC Official **Journal** C 227/94-101
25 _____ Doc. B 2-950/86
26 _____ Doc. B 2-948/86
27 _____ Doc. B 2-947/86
28 _____ Doc. B 21-951/86
29 _____ Doc. B 948/86
30 EC *Official Journal* C 297/55, 24 November 1986
31 _____ C297/39-40, 24 November 1986
32 _____ C297/52-54, 24 November 1986
33 _____ C297/56, 24 November 1986
34 _____ C297/55, 24 November 1986
35 _____ C297/4, 24 November 1986
36 European Parliament Doc. B 2-948/86, 22 October 1986
37 Barber 1980, p.80
38 Un General Assembly 23 September 1980
39 Conference of Foreign Ministers Communique, 22/23 July 1985
40 European Parliament, Doc A2-197/85, p.18
41 Holland 1987, p.300
42 EC Commission, Application of the EC Code of Conduct by Community companies with subsidiaries in South Africa: fifth summary analysis, 1985 p.11
43 European Parliament Doc. A2-197/85, p.22
44 Holland 1985 (A), p.13
45 Conference of Foreign Ministers, Statement on South Africa, 10 September 1985
46 Ibid.
47 Address to UN General Assembly, 24 September 1985, published in *Developments in the European Communities*, January 1986, pl-4046, p.125
48 European Report no. 1196, 5 February 1986
49 _____ no. 1190, 15 January 1986, p.5
50 European Council Communique 26–7 June 1986
51 Text of press conference 5 August 1986
52 European Report no. 1248, 10 September 1986
53 Conference of Foreign Ministers, Statement on South Africa, 17 September 1986
54 European Report no. 1251, 20 September 1986
55 Country Report, South Africa no. 4, 1986, p.16
56 Wallace 1983, p.14
57 Ibid. p.13
58 Ibid. p.14
59 Braun and Weiland 1987, p.17
60 European Council Communique 26–7 June 1986
61 Conference of Foreign Ministers, Statement on South Africa, 10 September 1985
62 Press statement issued in Brussels 24 April 1987
63 Ibid.
64 European Report no.1350 October 1987, p.2
65 Foot 1979, Lindemann 1982
66 Lindemann 1982, p.126
67 Foot 1979, p.357
68 Lindemann 1982, p.115

69 Barber 1986
70 SADCC conference on Investment in Production, February 1987
71 SADCC Report July 1986 — August 1987
72 Article 6, Lome Convention 1985
73 Joint Declaration, Annex 1, Lome III
74 *The Courier* no. 96, 1986
75 Goodison 1987, p.5
76 Hanlon and Omond 1987, pp.95-117
77 EC Commission *The European Community and Southern Africa*, December 1981, p.12
78 EC *Official Journal* C 10/37-9, 14 January 1987
79 _____ C 322/1157, 15 December 1986
80 313:78 in the House of Representatives and 78:21 in the Senate
81 Section 4, Public Law 99-440, 2 October 1986
82 Section 107.2
83 Law 99-440, 2 October 1986
84 Act Prohibiting Trade with the Republic of South Africa and Namibia 30 May 1986
85 *Dail Debates* 361:1072, 5 November 1985
86 Holland 1985 (B), p.415

Chapter Four: The Domestic Environment and Irish Policy towards South Africa

1 Central Bank of Ireland, Annual Report 1986, p.86
2 *Dail Debates* 226:1176, 15 February 1967
3 Stewart 1986, p.3
4 *Dail Debates* 363:2864, 10 February 1986
5 Stewart 1986
6 *Dail Debates* 203:983, 18 June 1963
7 _____ 251:2192, 25 February 1971
8 _____ 241:2278, 30 October 1969
9 _____ 301:18, 2 November 1977
10 _____ 327:2157, 24 March 1981
11 Press release, Department of Labour 27 May 1985
12 *Dail Debates* 361:685, 30 October 1985
13 *The Irish Times,* 18 June 1985
14 *Dail Debates* 362:355, 27 November 1985
15 _____ 362:1400, 15 December 1985
16 _____ 364:1679, 12 March 1986
17 Joint Trocaire/Irish Commission for Justice and Peace Statement 29 October 1985
18 Trocaire Press Release 29 October 1985
19 ICTU Press Release 6 September 1985
20 _____ 20 November 1985
21 Second Labour Court Report, unpublished
22 Bill 1985/86, 52 on the Prohibition of Imports of Agricultural Produce from South Africa, statement of reasons issued by the Ministry of Foreign Affairs, December 1985, p.24
23 *The Irish Times,* 20 December 1985
24 Labour Party Document, *Principles of International Policy,* paper 9, 1982
25 Letter of 8 January 1986, published in the *3rd Report of the Committee on Cooperation with Developing Countries,* 1986, p.55
26 Appendix 9, 3rd Report, Joint Committee on Cooperation with Developing Countries, p.61
27 SI no. 291 of 1986 p1.4317
28 Letter of 8 January 1986 published in *3rd Report of the Committee on Cooperation with Developing countries,* 1986, p.54
29 *Seanad Debates* 113:2239, 9 July 1986
30 Ibid.
31 *Sunday Independent,* 3 January 1988
32 *Africa South of the Sahara* 1988, p.978
33 IAAM Report 1978/79, p.11
34 Circular, *Contracts with South Africa and the Purchase of South African Produce,* 4 September 1984

35 *Dail Debates* 337:1045, 6 July 1982
36 ——————— 358:46, 7 May 1985
37 ——————— 362:1420, 5 December 1985
38 ——————— 214:755, 18 February 1965
39 ——————— 327:2162, 24 March 1981
40 *Southern Africa: Principles of International Policy,* Paper no.9 1982, p.22
41 Press statement 20 December 1985
42 ——————— 17 July 1986
43 ——————— 17 September 1986
44 Fine Gael manifesto 1987, p.71
45 Text of speech to Ard Fheis 17 October 1986
46 *Dail Debates* 373:19884, 16 June 1987
47 Wallace 1971, p.49
48 *Dail Debates* 307:116, 30 May 1978
49 ——————— 328:201, 25 March 1981
50 3rd Report, Committee on Cooperation with Developing Countries 1986, p.27
51 Ibid.
52 Ibid.
53 Sutton 1977, p.16
54 Annual Report on Assistance to Developing Countries 1986, p.27
55 3rd Report 1986, p.20

Chapter Five: Conclusions and Policy Recommendations

1 *Dail Debates* 178:29, 18 November 1959
2 ——————— 182:760, 8 June 1960
3 ——————— 302:1422, 14 December 1977
4 ——————— 306:370, 4 May 1978
5 *Financial Times,* 26 May 1987, p.3
6 MacKernan 1987, p.182
7 Keatinge 1983, p.151
8 Laffan 1983, p.107
9 Campaign for Irish Neutrality and Independence, *Citizens' Guide, Defence and Foreign Policy* 1987, p.9
10 *Dail Debates* 361:1073, 5 November 1985
11 ——————— 368:2224, 3 July 1986
12 ——————— 369: 533, 23 October 1986
13 Third Report, *Apartheid and Development in South Africa* 1986, p.31
14 *Dail Debates* 369:534, 23 October 1986
15 ——————— 371:153, 24 March 1987
16 ——————— 373:1884, 16 June 1987
17 Communique 18 October 1985, p.2
18 Keatinge 1983, p.144
19 *Seanad Debates* 113:2225, 9 July 1986
20 Keatinge 1978, p.222
21 Aberach et al., 1981, p.12
22 Brian Lenihan, Minister for Foreign Affairs, UN General Assembly, 25 September 1987, p.7
23 Orkin 1986, p.28
24 Burke 1775, Volume 4
25 Austin 1986, p.403
26 Orkin 1986, p.57
27 *The Observer,* 18 October 1987, p.8
28 Goodison 1987, p.5
29 IAAM Submission to the Oireachtas Committee on Cooperation with Developing Countries, Februry 1985, p.4
30 Third Report, 1986, p.26
31 'Why Third World Aid Should not be Cut', Trocaire Position Paper, November 1987, p.2
32 *The Times,* London, 19 October 1987
33 Fraser, Obasanjo 1986
34 *The Economist,* 22 August 1987, p.52
35 *Financial Times,* 28 October 1987

36 EC Commission Paper on Trade Developments with South Africa, 7 October 1987
37 Simon Report (draft), European Parliament, 7 July 1987, p.8
38 *Financial Times,* 16 June 1987
39 van der Ropp 1987, p.397
40 *AWEPAA News Bulletin* June 1987
41 Simon Report (draft), European Parliament, 7 July 1987, p.4
42 Minutes of Proceedings, European Parliament Resolution, 30 October 1987, p.11
43 Statement by the Taoiseach, Charles Haughey, Dail Debates 334:1426, 18 May 1982
44 Moorsom 1986, p.52
45 *Ireland's Official Development Assistance* 1986, p.55
46 Hanlon and Omond 1987, p.329
47 Becker 1987, p.160
48 Minutes of Proceedings, European Parliament Resolution, 30 October 1987, p.12
49 *The Guardian,* 2 October 1987
50 *Dail Debates* 2321, 4 November 1987
51 *The Guardian,* 2 October 1987
52 van der Ropp 1987, p.395
53 *Zulu Horizons* 1962, p.40

Appendices

SUMMARY OF WESTERN ECONOMIC SANCTIONS

	NEW INVESTMENTS	LOANS TO COMPANIES	LOANS TO SA GOVT	IMF LOANS	TRADE: General	Credits & Promotion	IMPORTS: Coal	Iron & Steel
Sec. Counc. Res. 566	to be stopped & apply disincentives							
Sec. Counc. Res. 569	to be suspended					susp. exp. loans guarantees		
Gen. Ass. Res. 40/64 I	to be stopped		to be stopped			end trade promotion		
NORDIC PROGRAM OF ACTION	prohibition or discouragement, incl. leasing & patents & manuf. licences		prohibition or discouragement	new loans to be opposed	find other suppliers & markets & no buying by (semi-)govt	no state support		
DENMARK	nordic & for Danes & subsidiaries outside country	included in investment ban	nordic	nordic			TOTAL	
FINLAND	nordic		banned	nordic	nordic		TOTAL	
ICELAND	nordic		nordic	nordic	nordic	nordic	TOTAL	
NORWAY	nordic prohibited	included in investment ban	banned	nordic			TOTAL	
SWEDEN	nordic, incl. for Swedes & subsidiaries outside country	included in investment ban	nordic	nordic			TOTAL	
JOINT EC POLICY	banned, but implementation pending							banned
European Parliament Res. 10-7-'86 and 22-10-'86	to be banned	new loans to be banned	new loans to be banned	new loans to be opposed	trade patterns to be monitored		to be banned	to be banned
BELGIUM	EC					lim. credit reinsurance		EC
DENMARK	see under Nordic Program of Action							
FRANCE	EC = no direct currency transfer					no new contracts		EC
F.R. GERMANY	EC					export credit limited		EC
GREECE	EC			opposed in '82				EC
IRELAND	EC & credit support ban			opposed in '82	(semi-)govt. buy non-SA			EC
ITALY	EC							EC
LUX'BOURG	EC							EC
NETHERLANDS	EC					limited credit reinsurance		EC
PORTUGAL	EC							EC
SPAIN	EC							EC
UNITED KINGDOM	EC = voluntary ban		no govt. to govt. loans					EC
COMMONWEALTH	to be banned, incl. profits reinvestment & govt. assistance	new bank loans to be banned	new bank loans to be banned		no govt. buying from SA	no govt. assistance, incl. for trade missions	to be banned	to be banned
AUSTRALIA	CW	CW	CW		CW & mutual trade missions closed	no export facilities	CW	CW
CANADA	CW	CW	CW		CW	ban on credit insurance	CW	CW
NEW ZEALAND	CW = legal ban considered	CW	CW		CW	CW	CW	CW
U.K.	see under European Community							
AUSTRIA	= EC					no credit guarantees		= EC
JAPAN	ban on direct investments		appeal to refrain			no trade prom & limited trade insurance		= EC
MALTA								
SWITZERL.				opposed '82				
UN. STATES OF AMERICA	banned, incl. providing assets	banned, except for trade finance	banned	new loans to be opposed	no import products S.A. (semi-)govt. companies	exp. subs. only if Sullivan code applied & no trade prom.	banned	banned

AGAINST SOUTH AFRICA

Gold Coins etc.	Agricultural Products	Strategic Minerals	Uranium imp. & Nucl Co-op.	OIL SUPPLY	COMPUTERS	AIR LINKS	MISCELLANEOUS
coin ban						re-examina-tion	re-examine maritime relations
coin ban			no new nucl. contracts		sale ban to army, police		
coin ban			nucl. co-op. to be ended	cessation of oil sale, export	sale ban to army, police, intelligence		
coin ban			**no new nuclear co-op.**		**sale ban to army, police**	**to be suspended**	**production in SA to be restricted**
T R A D E B A N			nordic	sale & transport on Danish-owned ships banned	nordic	SAS line suspended	nordic *(all measures Nam +)*
T R A D E B A N			nordic		nordic	nordic	nordic
nordic			nordic		nordic	nordic	nordic
T R A D E B A N			nordic	crude oil & products export banned & crude oil transport banned on nordic ships	nordic	SAS & other lines prohibited	nordic & ban organised tourist visits *(all Nam +)*
T R A D E B A N			nordic		nordic	SAS line suspended	nordic & maritime relations discouraged & local auth. boycott allowed *(all Nam +)*
coins banned			**no new nuclear co-op.**	**exp. ban domestic imported crude oil**	**no export to SA army & police**		*(all joint measures Nam.-)*
gold and gold coins to be banned	to be banned	alternative suppliers to be investigated	uranium ban & prohibit old & new nucl.co-op	exp. ban incl. products & bonded storage & technol. & finance & transp. & petrochemicals	exports to be banned	to be suspended	ban diamonds, textiles & purchases from SA govt.-owned comp. *(all measures Nam.+)*
EC			EC	EC, also products	EC		
EC			EC	EC	EC		
EC			EC	EC	EC		
EC			EC	EC & advise against calls at SA ports	EC		
EC	banned		EC	EC	EC		Bank of Ireland ends all business
EC			EC	EC	EC		
EC			EC	EC	EC		
EC & no SA gold in Ducate			EC	EC	EC		
EC			EC	EC	EC		
EC			EC	EC	EC	Iberia susp.	
			EC	UK crude oil only to Int. Energy Agency members	EC		vol. ban tourism promotion
preclude import Krugerrands	**to be banned**		**ur. ban & no new nuclear sales & exports**	**no sale & export to SA**	**no sale to mil.& police & security forces**	**to be banned**	**end double tax agreements & no govt. contracts SA firms & ban tourism promotion**
CW	CW		CW	CW = crude & products	CW	SAA banned after 1 year	CW
CW	CW		CW	CW = crude & products	CW	CW incl. cargo	CW
CW	CW		CW	CW	CW	CW	CW
		See under European Community					
= EC			= EC	= EC	= EC		
voluntary coin ban			= EC	= EC	= EC	no officials on SAA flights	no visa for SA tourists, Jap. visits discouraged
coins banned	**banned & textiles import**	**reduction investigated**	**uranium ban & nuclear equipment exp. restricted**	**crude & products export banned**	**banned if used for enforcement apartheid**	**banned**	**No SA (semi-) govt. deposits in US banks & double tax agreement** *(all Nam +)*

Source: AWEPAA, The Hague, May 1987 News Bulletin

Appendix B
Ireland's Allocation to UN Funds 1980–1985

Fund	£'000					
	1980	1981	1982	1983	1984	1985
UNTFSA	12,500	12,500	14,500	20,000	21,000	25,000
UNETPSA	12,500	12,500	14,500	20,000	21,000	25,000
UNFN	9,000	9,000	11,000	15,000	16,000	21,000
UNITAR	5,000	1,000	4,000	9,000	11,000	11,000
UNPFAA	–	–	1,000	1,000	1,000	1,000
TOTAL:	39,000	35,000	45,000	65,000	70,000	83,000

Key: UNTFSA-UN Trust Fund for South Africa, UNETPSA-UN Educational and Training Programme for Southern Africa, UNFN-UN Fund for Namibia, UNITAR-UN Institute for Training and Research, UNPFAA-UN Publicity Fund Against Apartheid

Source: 1980 and 1981-PQ 328: 472, 31 March 1981; Development Assistance Reports 1981–1985

Appendix C
UNGA Resolution on Concerted international action for the elimination of apartheid

The General Assembly:

Alarmed by the aggravation of the situation in South Africa caused by the policy of *apartheid*, and lately, in particular, by the reimposition of the state of emergency and its extension nation-wide,

Convinced that the root-cause of the crisis in southern Africa is the policy of *apartheid*,

Noting with grave concern that in order to perpetuate *apartheid* in South Africa the authorities there have increasingly committed acts of aggression and breaches of the peace,

Convinced that only the total eradication of *apartheid* and the establishment of majority rule on the basis of the free and fair exercise of universal adult suffrage can lead to a peaceful and lasting solution in South Africa,

Noting that the so-called reforms in South Africa have the effect of further entrenching the *apartheid* system and further dividing the people of South Africa,

Recognizing that the policy of bantustanization deprives the majority of the people of their citizenship and makes them foreigners in their own country,

Recognizing the responsibility of the United Nations and the international community to take all necessary action for the eradication of *apartheid*, and, in particular, the need for increased and effective pressure on the South African authorities as a peaceful means of achieving the abolition of *apartheid*,

Encouraged, in this context, by the growing international consensus, as demonstrated by the adoption of Security Council resolution 569 (1985) of 26 July 1985, and the increase in the expansion of national, regional and intergovernmental measures to this end,

Taking note of the Declaration adopted by the World Conference on Sanctions against Racist South Africa.[1]

Convinced of the vital importance of the strict observance of Security Council resolution 418 (1977) of 4 November 1977, by which the Council instituted a mandatory arms embargo against South Africa, and Security Council resolution 558 (1984) of 13 December 1984 concerning the import of arms, ammunition and military vehicles produced in South Africa, and of the need to make these embargoes fully effective.

Commending the national policies not to sell and export oil to South Africa,

Considering that measures to ensure effective and scrupulous implementation of such embargoes through international co-operation are essential and urgent,

Noting with deep concern that, through a combination of military and economic pressures, in violation of international law, the authorities of South Africa have increasingly resorted to economic reprisals and aggression against, and destabilization of the neighbouring States,

Considering that contacts between *apartheid* South Africa and the front-line and other neighbouring States, necessitated by geography, colonial legacy and other reasons, should not be used by other States as a pretext for legitimizing the *apartheid* system or justifying attempts to break the international isolation of that system,

Convinced that the existence of *apartheid* will continue to lead to ever-increasing resistance by the oppressed people, by all possible manner, and increased tension and conflict that will have far-reaching consequences for southern Africa and the world,

Convinced that policies of collaboration with the *apartheid* régime, instead of respect for the legitimate aspirations of the genuine representatives of the great majority of the people, will encourage its repression and aggression against neighbouring States and defiance of the United Nations,

Expressing its full support for the legitimate aspiration of African States and peoples, and of the Organization of African Unity, for the total Liberation of the continent of Africa from colonialism and racism,

1. *Strongly condemns* the policy of *apartheid* which deprives the majority of the South African population of their citizenship, fundamental freedoms and human rights;
2. *Strongly condemns* the South African authorities for the killings, arbitrary mass arrests and the detention of members of mass organizations as well as individuals, the overwhelming majority of whom belong to the majority population, for opposing the *apartheid* system and the state of emergency;
3. *Further condemns* the overt and the covert aggressive actions, which South Africa has increasingly carried out for the destabilization of neighbouring States, as well as those aimed against refugees from South Africa and Namibia;
4. *Demands* that the authorities of South Africa:
   (*a*) Release immediately and unconditionally Nelson Mandela and all other political prisoners, detainees and restrictees;
   (*b*) Immediately lift the state of emergency;
   (*c*) Abrogate discriminatory laws and lift bans on all organizations and individuals, as well as end restrictions on and censorship of news media;
   (*d*) Grant freedom of association and full trade union rights to all workers of South Africa;
   (*e*) Initiate without pre-conditions a political dialogue with genuine leaders of the majority population with a view to eradicating *apartheid* without delay and establishing a representative government;
   (*f*) Eradicate the bantustan structures;
   (*g*) Immediately withdraw all their troops from southern Angola and end the destabilization of front-line and other States;
5. *Urges* the Security Council to consider without delay the adoption of effective mandatory sanctions against South Africa;
6. *Further urges* the Security Council to take steps for the strict implementation of the mandatory arms embargo instituted by it in resolution 418 (1977) and of the arms embargo requested in its resolution 558 (1984) and, within the context of the relevant resolutions, to secure an end to military and nuclear co-operation with

South Africa and the import of military equipment or supplies from South Africa;

7. *Appeals* to all States that have not yet done so, pending mandatory sanctions by the Security Council, to consider national legislative or other appropriate measures to increase the pressure on the *apartheid* régime of South Africa, such as:

(a) Cessation of further investment in, and financial loans to, South Africa;

(b) An end to all promotion of and support for trade with South Africa;

(c) Prohibition of the sale of Krugerrand and all other coins minted in South Africa;

(d) Cessation of all forms of military, police or intelligence co-operation with the authorities of South Africa, in particular the sale of computer equipment;

(e) An end to nuclear collaboration with South Africa;

(f) Cessation of export and sale of oil to South Africa;

8. *Appeals* to all States, organizations and institutions recognizing the pressing need, existing and potential, of South Africa's neighbouring States for economic assistance:

(a) To increase assistance to the front-line States and the Southern African Development Co-ordination Conference in order to increase their economic strength and independence from South Africa;

(b) To increase humanitarian, legal, educational and other assistance and support to the victims of *apartheid*, to the liberation movements recognized by the Organization of African Unity and to all those struggling against *apartheid* and for a non-racial, democratic society in South Africa;

9. *Appeals* to all Governments and organizations to take appropriate action for the cessation of all academic, cultural, scientific and sports relations that would support the *apartheid* régime of South Africa, as well as relations with individuals, institutions and other bodies endorsing or based on *apartheid*;

10. *Commends* those States that have already adopted voluntary measures against the *apartheid* régime of South Africa in accordance with General Assembly resolution 40/64 I of 10 December 1985 and invites those that have not yet done so to follow their example;

11. *Reaffirms* the legitimacy of the struggle of the oppressed people of South Africa for the total eradication of *apartheid* and for the establishment of a non-racial, democratic society in which all the people, irrespective of race, colour or creed, enjoy fundamental freedoms and human rights;

12. *Pays tribute to and expresses solidarity with* organizations and individuals struggling against *apartheid* and for a non-racial, democratic society in accordance with the principles of the Universal Declaration of Human Rights.[2]

13. *Requests* the Secretary-General to report to the General Assembly at its forty-second session on the implementation of the present resolution.

---

1 *Report of the World Conference on Sanctions against Racist South Africa*, Paris, 16-20 June 1986 (United Nations publication, Sales No. E.86.I.23), sect. IX. See also A/41/424-S/18185 and Corr. 1, annex.

2 General Assembly resolution 217 A (III).

Appendix D
International Convention Against Apartheid in Sport

Article 3

States Parties shall not permit sports contact with a country practising *apartheid* and shall take appropriate action to ensure that their sports bodies, sports teams and individual sportsmen do not have such contact.

Article 6

Each State Party shall take appropriate action against its sports bodies, teams and individual sportsmen that participate in sports activities in a country practising *apartheid*, which, in particular, shall include:

(*a*) Refusal to provide financial or other assistance for any purpose to such sports bodies, teams and individual sportsmen;

(*b*) Restriction of access to national sports facilities to such sports bodies, teams and individual sportsmen;

(*c*) Non-enforceability of all sports contracts which involve sports activities in a country practising *apartheid* or with teams or individual sportsmen selected on the basis of *apartheid*;

(*d*) Denial and withdrawal of national honours or awards in sports to such teams and individual sportsmen;

(*e*) Denial of official receptions in honour of such teams or sportsmen.

Article 10

1. States Parties shall use their best endeavours to ensure universal compliance with the Olympic principle of non-discrimination and the provisions of this Convention.

2. Towards this end, States Parties shall prohibit entry into their countries of members of teams and individual sportsmen participating or who have participated in sports competitions in South Africa and shall prohibit entry into their countries of representatives of sports bodies, members of teams and individual sportsmen who invite on their own initiative sports bodies, teams and sportsmen officially representing a country practising *apartheid* and participating under its flag. States Parties may also prohibit entry of representatives of sports bodies, members of teams or individual sportsmen who maintain sports contacts with sports bodies, teams or sportsmen representing a country practising *apartheid* and participating under its flag. Prohibition of entry should not violate the regulations of the relevant sports federations which support the elimination of *apartheid* in sports and shall apply only to participation in sports activities.

3. States Parties shall advise their national representatives to international sports' federations to take all possible and practical steps to prevent the participation of the sports bodies, teams and sportsmen referred to in paragraph 2 above in international sports competitions and shall, through their representatives in international sports organizations, take every possible measure to:

(*a*) Ensure the expulsion of South Africa from all federations in which it still holds membership as well as to deny South Africa reinstatement to membership of any federation from which it has been expelled; and

(*b*) In case of national federations condoning sports exchanges with a country practising *apartheid*, to impose sanctions against such national federations including, if necessary, expulsion from the relevant international sports organization and exclusion of its representatives from participation in international sports competitions.

4. In cases of flagrant violations of the provisions of this Convention, States Parties shall take appropriate action as they deem fit, including where necessary steps aimed at the exclusion of the responsible national sports governing bodies, national sports federations or sportsmen of the countries concerned from international sports competition.

5. The provisions of the present article relating specifically to South Africa shall cease to apply when the system of *apartheid* is abolished in that country.

Source: International Conventions against Apartheid in Sports, adopted by United Nations General Assembly, December 1985

Appendix E
EC (12) Exports to South Africa by Principal Product and Exporter, 1986

Product	Value (in 1,000 ECUs)	Main Exporter	
Machinery, Mechanical Parts	1,189,942	FRG	43.6%
Notably			
— computers	249,666		
— Internal Combustion Engines	111,598		
— Nuclear Reactors	51,096		
Motor Vehicles and Parts	550,231	FRG	80.0%
		UK	13.6%
		I	3.6%
Electrical Equipment	517,393	FRG	46.3%
		UK	23.1%
		F	14.1%
Plastics	200,165	FRG	47.6%
		UK	17.8%
		N/lands	8.9%

Source: Eurostat, Nimexe External Trade, Vols J and Z, 1986.

Appendix F
EC (12) Imports from South Africa by Principal Product and Importer, 1986

Product	Value (in 1,000 ECU's)	Main Importer	
Diamonds	1,846,432	Belg./Lux	99.9%
Gold	1,625,577	I	85.2%
		FRG	13.2%
Minerals	875,987	I	25.3%
		FRG	21.0%
		Spain	16.8%
Coal	828,365	I	26.4%
Fruit & Vegetables	325,218	UK	44.7%
		FRG	23.5%
		F	16.9%
Metallic Ores	347,540	UK	48.3%
		FRG	14.9%
		I	11.1%
Wool	205,523	UK	27.5%
		FRG	22.8%
		I	19.6%
Copper	196,921	FRG	45.2%
		Belg./Lux	27.3%
		I	13.7%
Ferro Alloys	190,475	FRG	40.2%
		F	21.7%
		I	16.1%
Chemical Products	150,301	F	55.6%
		FRG	16.4%
		N/lands	11.6%
Gold Coins	90,570	FRG	79.5%
		Belg./Lux	20.5%

Source: Eurostat, Nimexe External Trade, 1986, Vols B, G, H and Z

	Chromium (total Cr)	Ferro-chromium	Manganese ore	Ferro-manganese
Percentage of world production by				
South Africa	31	31	15	7
USSR	35	15	36	31
South Africa's share (%) of imports by:				
United States	54	63	28	45
EEC	51	39	44	52
Japan	45	63	49	0

	Platinum group metals	Vanadium	Gold
Percentage of world production by:			
South Africa	53	38	48
USSR	41	29	19
South Africa's share (%) of imports by:			
United States	64		
EEC	47		
Japan	49		

Production figures are for 1984. South Africa and the USSR occupy first or second place for six of the minerals. For ferro-manganese, the USSR is number 1 and South Africa number 4. Import figures are for 1980-84 (US) and 1980-83 (EEC and Japan), and include both direct and indirect imports.

Source: *South Africa and Critical Minerals*, Open File Report 1976-86, Bureau of Mines, US Department of Interior, July 1986

Appendix H
Lome Aid (I & II) to Southern Africa Disbursed 1975-85

	1,000 ECU Lome I	Lome II
Botswana	23.2	10.1
Lesotho	21.0	16.4
Malawi	71.1	28.9
Swaziland	27.8	14.5
Zambia	63.4	72.6
Zimbabwe	—	24.6
Tanzania	122.8	73.8
TOTAL	329.3	240.9

Source: Ten Years of Lome, EC Commission, September 1986, p.78.

Appendix I
Ireland's Imports of Fruit and Vegetables from South Africa
1980-86

	Amount (£m)	% of Total Imports from South Africa	% of Total Imports of Fruit and Vegetables
1980	5,669	48	5.7
1981	4,334	40	3.5
1982	6,244	47	4.2
1983	4,109	32	2.8
1984	5,447	31	3.1
1985	5,340	26	3.0
1986	3,707	23	2.0

Source: Trade Statistics of Ireland, CSO 1980–1986

Appendix J
Ireland's Imports of Coal from South Africa 1980-86

Year	Amount (£m)	% of Total Imports from South Africa	% of Total Coal Imports
1980	0.677	6	1.1
1981	1.071	10	1.2
1982	0.597	4	0.7
1983	1.698	13	1.8
1984	1.541	9	1.6
1985	4.988	24	3.5
1986	2.903	18	1.8

Source: Trade Statistics of Ireland, CSO 1980—1986

Appendix K
Ireland's Exports of Computers to South Africa 1980-86

Year	£m	% of Total Exports of Computers
1980	0.232	0.1
1981	1.286	0.4
1982	4.166	0.9
1983	4.730	0.7
1984	5.858	0.5
1985	5.874	0.5
1986	8.278	0.6

Source: Trade Statistics of Ireland Series, CSO 1980—1986

Appendix L
Dail Questions on South Africa 1959-86

Dr. N. Browne	Ind/Lab	34
Mr. R. Quinn	Lab	22
Mr. B. Desmond	Lab	19
Mr. P. de Rossa	WP	17
Mr. J. McQuillan	NPD	10
Mr. R. Ryan	FG	9
Mr. G. Collins	FF	7
Mr. N. Andrews	FF	6
Mr. N. Lemass	FF	6
Mr. B. Corish	Lab	5
Mr. T. MacGiolla	WP	5
Mr. J. O'Keeffe	FG	5
Dr. G. FitzGerald	FG	4
Mr. M. O'Kennedy	FF	3
Mr. D. Desmond	Lab	3
Mr. B. Ahearn	FF	2
Mr. T. Gregory	Ind	2
Dr. J. O'Connell	Lab/FF	2
Mr. M. O'Leary	Lab/FG	2
Mr. M. Taylor	Lab	2
Mr. M. Bell	Lab	1
Mr. S. Brennan	FF	1
Mr. L. Cosgrave	FG	1
Mr. S. Doherty	FF	1
Mr. O. J. Flanagan	FG	1
Mr. M. D. Higgins	Lab	1
Mr. J. Horgan	Lab	1
Mr. E. Kenny	FG	1
Mr. B. Lenihan	FF	1
Mr. T. Lynch	FG	1
Mr. M. Manning	FG	1
Mr. A. Millar	FF	1
Mr. G. Mitchell	FG	1
Mr. S. Moore	FF	1
Dr. C. C. O'Brien	Lab	1
Mrs. N. Owen	FG	1
Mr. A. Shatter	FG	1
Dr. D. Thornley	Lab	1
Mr. J. Wilson	FF	1
Dr. M. Woods	FF	1
TOTALS 40		**185**

Appendix M
Official Development Assistance from Ireland to Priority Countries 1981-85

Country	1981	1982	(£'000) 1983	1984	1985
Lesotho	1,737	2,427	2,429	2,790	2,397
Tanzania	480	917	1,511	1,768	2,078
Zambia	404	813	904	876	1,836
Sudan	756	272	398	359	878
TOTAL	3,377	4,429	5,242	5,793	7,189

Source: Ireland-Assistance to Developing Countries 1981—1985

Glossary of Terms with related Abbreviations

African National Congress (ANC) Founded in 1912, the ANC, is the oldest liberation movement in Africa. Its original membership came largely from the black Christian elite, including chiefs and intellectuals. It has included a wide spectrum of opinion since its formation. The ANC was banned in 1960 after a series of campaigns in defiance of racist laws. After over half a century of non-violent resistance, the ANC formed a military wing 'Umkhonto we Sizwe' (Spear of the Nation). In 1955, the ANC, with three other organisations drew up the Freedom Charter which remains its basic document for a post-apartheid South Africa. It calls for a multiracial democracy in which 'all national groups shall have equal rights'. (Reprinted in full in Commonwealth Group of Eminent Persons, *Mission to South Africa*, Penguin 1986).

Afrikaner Used to describe the Dutch settlers who first colonised southern Africa in 1652. After the Boer War (1899–1902), when the Afrikaner settlers were defeated by the British, they adopted a rigid nationalism which developed into a systematic and legalised oppression of the black majority.

Arms Embargo In 1977, the UN Security Council adopted Resolution 418 which prohibits the sale of arms and related equipment to South Africa.

Association of West European Parliamentarians for Action Against Apartheid (AWEPAA) An association, based in the Hague, of parliamentarians in national parliaments and the European Parliament who campaign against apartheid.

African, Caribbean and Pacific (ACP) Used to describe the third world states who participate in the Lome Convention.

Azanian People's Organisation (AZAPO) Appeared in 1978 as the successor to the 'Black Consciousness' movement of the early 1970's.

Bantustan Structures The Bantustan policy is a central component of apartheid; all Africans were assigned to one or other of the homelands (for example Transkei, Ciskei, Boputhatswana). The purpose is to confine all of the blacks to a limited area of land. As a result of becoming a citizen of one of the homelands, a person loses South African citizenship.

Bantu Education In 1955, the South African Parliament passed the Bantu Education Act which provided a separate and inferior education for black children.

Black Consciousness This movement came to the fore in the 1970s emphasising the need for black people to organise together as blacks with a view to psychological liberation and self-help.

Code of Conduct In 1978 the European Community adopted a voluntary code of conduct for EC multinationals operating in South Africa with the objective of breaking down segregation in the workplace and improving the working conditions of black workers. The Code was revised and strengthened in 1985.

Commonwealth A loose international grouping of former British colonies and the United Kingdom.

Comprehensive Sanctions Usually applied to sanctions that impose a total economic boycott on a state. All economic links are cut off.

Communique Text of statement issued after meetings of EC and EPC institutions.

Communist Party of South Africa (CPSA) Founded in 1921, the CPSA initially concentrated on penetrating the white craft unions. Soon, however, it focussed on black members in the trade unions and the African National Congress, and by the late 1940s was campaigning for a single, non-racial state. It was banned in 1950.

Conference of Foreign Ministers Meetings in European Political Cooperation (EPC) between Foreign Ministers of the European Community.

Congress of South African Trade Unions (COSATU) Established on 1 December 1985 with 24 affiliated trade unions. It is based on the principles of non-racialism, worker control, one union member per industry, national cooperation.

Conservative Party Represents part of the white electorate in South Africa and is to the right of the National Party. Following the May 1987 election it became the official opposition party.

Constructive Engagement Term used to describe US policy towards South Africa during the Reagan Administration's first term. It involved increased dialogue with the South African Government. Pressure from the Anti-Apartheid Movement and Congress has forced a change in policy. In 1986 the US imposed wide-ranging sanctions against South Africa.

COREUR Network Direct telex link between the Foreign Ministries of the EC. It provides a system of immediate communication between the Foreign Ministries.

Demarche A formal diplomatic note.

Disinvestment Sale of direct investment holdings in South African commercial and industrial enterprises.

Dunnes Stores Strike In 1984 a worker in a Dublin branch of Dunnes Stores refused to check out South African fruit. She was suspended and a protracted strike ensued which led to a unilateral ban by Ireland on the importation of South African fruit and vegetables.

Eminent Persons Group In October 1985 the Commonwealth decided to establish a small group of 'eminent persons' who would go to South Africa to meet with representatives of the Government and the black and coloured populations in an effort to initiate a dialogue for change.

European Community (EC) Describes a number of different international organisations between twelve of the countries of Western Europe — the European Coal and Steel Community, the European Economic Community, and EURATOM.

European Council Twice yearly meetings between the Heads of Government and State of the countries of the European Community.

European Economic Community (EEC) Based on the Rome Treaty, the EEC was set up in 1958 to establish a customs union and a common market among a number of West European countries.

European Democratic Group (EDG) A party grouping in the European Parliament which mainly represents the British Conservative Party.

European Parliament Working Document The European Parliament does most of its work in committees which produce working documents. EP Resolutions are usually based on a background report originating in one or other of the committees.

European People's Party (EPP) A transnational party consisting of Christian Democratic parties in the European Parliament.

European Political Cooperation (EPC) A form of cooperation between EC countries in the area of foreign policy. The process began in 1979 and was formally institutionalised in the Single European Act of 1986.

EPC Secretariat The Single European Act made provision for the establishment of a small secretariat located in Brussels to service EPC meetings.

Explanations of Vote (EOV) In the UN General Assembly, countries have developed a practice of issuing an EOV concerning their votes on Resolutions.

Fianna Fail Largest political party in Ireland.

Fine Gael Second largest political party in Ireland.

Frontline States Those countries which border on South Africa or are part of Southern Africa (Botswana, Angola, Zambia, Zimbabwe, Malawi, Swaziland, Lesotho).

General Agreement on Tariffs and Trade (GATT) After the Second World War multilateral negotions were held to establish regulatory institutions for the world economy. The GATT entered into force on 1 January 1948 and is designed to provide a framework for the negotiation of reductions in barriers to trade.

The Hague Measures Sanctions adopted by the European Community in September 1986 following a European Council Meeting at the Hague in July 1986.

Homelands see above under Bantustan structures.

Inkatha Launched as a Zulu Cultural Association in 1975 by Chief Gatsha Buthelezi, Prime Minister of the KwaZulu bantustan. Chief Buthelezi has refused to accept independence for KwaZulu. He is firmly opposed to the use of economic sanctions against South Africa.

International Court of Justice The principle judicial organ of the UN. Its role and function are set out in the Charter.

International Monetary Fund (IMF) The IMF was established in 1945 together with the World Bank. The function of the IMF is to promote international monetary cooperation and exchange rate stability. It has the power to issue loans to countries in balance of payments difficulties

Irish Anti-Apartheid Movement (IAAM) Founded in 1964 as a non-party political and and non-sectarian organisation campaigning for independence and liberation in Southern Africa and against apartheid.

Irish Commission for Justice and Peace Established in 1970 by the Irish Episcopal Conference as a sign of the involvement of the Irish Catholic Church in the struggle for justice and peace in Ireland and throughout the world. Promotes study, research, education and action programmes in various aspects of peace, justice, human rights and world development.

Irish Congress of Trade Unions (ICTU) The central authority for the trade union movement in Ireland with 83 unions affiliated.

Irish Rugby Football Union (IRFU) The representative body for amateur competitive rugby in Ireland.

Kagiso Trust Founded in 1986, it acts as one of the channels for the transfer of EEC funds to South Africa out of the Special Fund for the victims of apartheid. It relates to projects and programmes which would not normally fall within the remit of the South African Catholic Bishops' Conference or the South African Council of Churches which are the other two channels.

Krugerrands South African gold coins.

Likeminded Describes a country's stance in international politics when it is congruent with another's. The "Likeminded Group" was set up in 1975 as a forum for Development Ministers from 10 industrialised countries to meet informally to discuss North/South issues.

The Lome Convention A wide-ranging convention originally signed in 1975 between the countries of the European Community and a large number of developing countries in Africa, the Caribbean and the Pacific (ACP). The Third Lome Convention is at present in operation.

Mandatory Sanctions Sanctions of this kind may be passed by the UN Security Council under the terms of the Charter.

Namibia Namibia, a territory of 824,000 sq. kms. in south-west Africa, was made a mandated territory by the League of Nations in 1920 after the colonial power (Germany) was defeated in the First World War. South Africa was given a trusteeship of Namibia by the League of Nations in 1920. In 1966 the UN General Assembly terminated South Africa's mandate and called for its complete withdrawal from Namibia. In 1971 the International Court of Justice upheld the General Assembly's mandate revocation. South Africa has refused to accept the UN as the legal heir of the League of Nations and has refused to withdraw from Namibia.

National Party Dominates political life in South Africa and has held power since 1948. It adheres rigidly to the principles of racial separation and has imposed severe restrictions on blacks through its policies of homelands, pass laws and draconian detention laws.

Non-governmental Organization (NGO) In this study NGO refers to Third World Development organisations funded from non official sources.

Nordic Cooperation There is a long history of cooperation between the Scandinavian countries on economic and political issues. Nordic Ministers meeting in February 1948 established a Joint Nordic Committee for Economic Cooperation which led to the Nordic Council. The signing of the Helsinki Convention in March 1962 by the five Nordic states (Denmark, Sweden, Norway, Finland and Iceland) codified Nordic cooperation.

Pan-Africanist Congress Banned with the ANC in 1960, this breakaway group has been eclipsed by the ANC in the last decade.

Partial sanctions Sanctions that affect a limited range of products.

Political Committee Part of the structure of European Political Cooperation (EPC). The Committee services meetings at Foreign Ministers' level.

Possible Negotiating Concept Developed by the Eminent Persons Group as the basis for a dialogue between the black majority and the South African government. Following discussions with the government the EPG concluded that it was not prepared to negotiate.

Presidency All member states of the European Community hold the Presidency of the Community for a period of six months in rotation. The Presidency is responsible for organising the schedule of Council meetings and for representing the Community in many international fora.

Progressive Federal Party The most liberal of the prominent white parties and now open to other races.

Sharpeville On 21 March 1960, several thousand protestors gathered in Sharpeville to march on local police stations and return their pass books. Police opened fire on the protestors killing 69 people and wounding some 180 others.

Single European Act (SEA) Signed in early 1986 and ratified after a referendum in Ireland in May 1987. It was the outcome of an Intergovernmental Conference convened by the EC Member States to negotiate changes to the Rome Treaty. The SEA introduces new areas of cooperation, develops existing common policies, involves a number of institutional changes and codifies European Political Cooperation.

Southern African Development Coordination Conference (SADCC) SADCC formally came into being in Lusaka (1980) with the primary objective of reducing the region's dependence on South Africa. It has nine members (Angola, Botswana, Lesotho, Malawi, Mozambique, Swaziland, Tanzania, Zambia, and Zimbabwe) and operates on the basis of sectoral development programmes, notably, transport and communication, food security, industry and trade, and mining.

Soweto On 16 June 1976, in Soweto some 20,000 schoolchildren marched in protest against a Government decision that Afrikaans (language of the ruling Afrikaner minority) would be one of the required languages of instruction in black secondary schools. The police opened fire on the students killing four of them. A period of 16 months of unrest followed.

Trocaire The Catholic Agency for World Development, set up by the Roman Catholic Bishops of Ireland in 1973, to express the Church's concern for the needs and problems of the people of developing countries and the principles of social justice involved. Its principal activities are a development co-operation programme of medium and long term projects in the Third World; a development education programme designed to generate greater awareness in Ireland of the problems and needs of the Third World; and emergency relief programmes in times of disasters.

United Democratic Front (UDF) Formed in 1983 to co-ordinate black demands for democracy, the UDF was active in fighting the new South African Constitution in 1983. Following the declaration of the state of emergency in July 1985, the top leadership of the UDF was arrested.

United Nations Charter In June 1945, 50 countries met in San Francisco to adopt the UN Charter. The Charter consists of 18 Chapters and 111 Articles setting out the role and functions of the UN and its institutions.

United Nations Convention on the Suppression and Punishment of the Crime of Apartheid Adopted by the General Assembly in 1973, it entered into force in 1976. It declares apartheid to be a crime against humanity and states that inhuman acts resulting from such a policy are crimes that violate the principles of international law and the UN Charter.

United Nations General Assembly All members of the UN are members of the General Assembly. The Assembly has no power to compel any Government to take any action. Its influence is exercised by the weight of its recommendations as an expression of world opinion. The Assembly meets once a year in regular session and there is provision for special sessions. A large number of committees service the work of the General Assembly.

United Nations Security Council The Security Council is composed of five permanent members (China, France, the Soviet Union, the United Kingdom and the United States) and ten non-permanent members elected by the General Assembly for two-year terms. The Security Council alone has the power to take decisions which all Member States are obligated under the Charter to accept and carry out. The Security Council operates on the basis of majority vote and any of the 5 permanent members can veto a resolution.

United Nations Special Committee Against Apartheid Estabished in 1962 by the General Assembly, the Committee is active in the fight against apartheid.

UN Western European and Other Group One of the General Assembly groups which organises representation on the committees of the General Assembly. It has no role in policy.

Unilateral Measures Term used to describe measures taken by one country against South Africa.

Ultimate Consignee A declaration is required from the ultimate consignee of computer products exported by Ireland to South Africa that the goods are not for use by the South African security forces.

A Brief History of Apartheid

History

Apartheid is an Afrikaans word meaning 'separateness'. It was first introduced as government policy in South Africa in 1948. 'The system of enforced racial separation known as apartheid forms the basis for the political, economic, and social dominance of South Africa by the white minority.'[1] The Afrikaners, descendants of the Dutch settlers who had colonised Southern Africa from the mid-17th century, had been defeated by the British in the Boer War of 1899–1902.

Thereafter, in pursuit of political supremacy in South Africa and a share of the economic gains monopolised by the British, the Afrikaner leaders realized that they would need the support of the white working class. They therefore paid considerable attention to the condition of the poor whites in the cities and cultivated a narrow nationalism based on race, language and religion; for example exhorting Afrikaners to support Afrikaner shopkeepers, firms etc. The National Party, founded in 1914 reflected the concerns of the Afrikaners. It promoted measures to protect white workers and the white poor from African competition, such as splitting trade unions along racial lines. Poor whites were convinced that their own security depended on white supremacy and nationalist unity was cemented.

The 1910 constitution, which created the South African state enshrined racial differences, and many racially discriminatory laws and practices were in place prior to 1948. But in that year the (Afrikaner) National Party came to power promising to codify and systematise existing segregation into a policy of 'separate development' for whites, blacks, Indians, and coloureds (of mixed race). The more rigid segregation in housing, education and other social policies came to be known as 'petty apartheid'. In the early 1960's a parallel policy of 'grand apartheid' began which divided the country into separate 'homelands' for blacks. 'Under this policy, all black Africans (representing over 74 percent of the population) were permanently denied political and residential rights in 'white' areas comprising some 87 percent of South Africa's total land area, including the areas richest in natural resources and development infrastructure.'[2] Four of the ten so-called homelands — Transkei, Boputhatswana, Venda and Ciskei — have been declared independent by South Africa, but no other country has recognized them as independent.

Successive National Party governments have enacted laws to limit the rights and opportunities of blacks and restrict relations between different racial groups. A recent US State Department Report summarises them as follows:

— the Population Registration Act of 1950, requiring classification of all South Africans on the basis of race;
— the Group Areas Act of 1950, providing that certain designated areas could be owned or inhabited only by people of specified races and requiring that residential areas be segregated on the basis of race;
— the Black (Urban Areas) Consolidation Act of 1945, the Black Labour Act of 1964, and the Black Labour Regulations, which, along with other laws and regulations, established a system of 'influx control' regulating the entrance and employment of blacks in white areas of the country and restricting the residence of blacks to the segregated townships established near white areas;
— the Native (Abolition of Passes and Coordination of Documents) Act of 1952, providing that police and other authorised government personnel could at any time demand the production of a 'pass' to enforce influx control restrictions;
— the Promotion of Bantu Self-Government Act of 1959, providing for the creation of separate (and potentially 'independent') national states or 'homelands' for each of the designated black ethnic groups;
— the Bantu Homelands Citizenship Act of 1970, making every black South African a citizen of one of the ethnic homelands, including millions of blacks who had always lived in white areas and had no ties with any of the designated homeland areas;
— the Reservation of Separate Amenities Act of 1953, establishing the requirement that separate buildings and services were to be reserved for different racial groups;
— the Prohibition of Mixed Marriages Act of 1949 and the Immorality Amendments Act of 1957, prohibiting marriages and sexual relations between whites and members of other racial groups;
— the Bantu Education Act of 1953, placing education of blacks under the separate control of the Department of Native Affairs and directing that black children receive an education markedly different from (and in practice vastly inferior to) that received by white children;
— the Native Labour (Settlement of Disputes) Act of 1953 and the Industrial Conciliation Amendment Act of 1956, prohibiting blacks from joining registered (i.e. officially recognised) unions and authorising the reservation of industrial jobs for members of specified races.

Finally, under the Public Safety Act of 1953 the government is empowered to declare a State of Emergency in specified areas or over the whole country for up to twelve months. This was used most recently in 1986 when a nationwide State of Emergency was declared. This was extended for a further 12 months in June 1987.

Emergency regulations are used to suspend a wide range of laws; to restrict and suppress the press; to permit the police to arrest and detain persons without a warrant; to conduct warrantless searches and seizures; and to give police complete immunity from prosecution for their actions.[3]

Between the declaration of the State of Emergency in June 1986 and January 1987 over 20,000 people were detained. Most of them were denied access to their families and legal counsel and many have been tortured. In April 1987, the Commissioner of Police announced that over 4,000 people were still being detained under the emergency legislation of whom 1,424 were 18 years old or younger.[4]

The US State Department summed up the intent and effect of the apartheid laws in limiting the economic and educational development of black South Africans as follows:

Apartheid has constrained the movement, residence, and employment of every black in South Africa. Between 1975 and 1984, over 1.9 million blacks were arrested for pass law and influx control violations. Between 1960 and 1983, over 3.5 million blacks were relocated by the government. Many of these relocations have been conducted forcibly. Most relocations have been to the impoverished and increasingly overcrowded homelands, where educational, health, and other essential services are grossly inadequate and employment opportunities severely limited. As a result of these relocations, thousands of blacks work as 'temporary' migrants in urban areas and are separated from their families for months and even years at a time.'[5]

This is despite the programme of reforms introduced since 1978, which has left the main pillars of apartheid untouched. The new constitution introduced in 1983, for example, granted limited national political rights to Coloureds and Asians, but the government of South Africa steadfastly refuses to even consider granting full political rights at the national level to blacks.

The Plight of Blacks in South Africa

Blacks comprise 74% of the population of South Africa (including the 'independent' homelands). Whites make up 14.7%; Coloureds 8.6% and Asians 2.7%.

Extreme disparities of income, wealth, and living conditions exist between the black and white population. For example,

— As of 1975, the designated ethnic 'homelands' (8 at that time) officially accounted for roughly 35 percent of South Africa's total population, but produced only 3 percent of total output.

— Although whites constituted less than 20 percent of the population, they consumed between 56 and 61 percent of the goods and services financed by the government between 1949-50 and 1975-76.

— In 1980, whites (who made up 16 percent of the population at the time) received 60 percent of total personal income, while blacks (72 percent of the population) received only 29 percent of total personal income. In 1970, the personal income shares received by the two groups were 72 and 19 percent respectively.

— Among countries classified by the World Bank as being in the upper portion of the middle-income category, only Algeria and Iran had higher infant mortality and child death rates than South Africa. The South African rates in both of these categories were at least double the rates in 14 out of the 20 countries in this classification.[6]

A major study of poverty in South Africa carried out by the University of Cape Town and funded by the Carnegie Corporation from 1982 to 1984 found that:

— in percentage terms more children under the age of one die each year in South Africa than in Mozambique, Cuba or Mexico;

— one-third of black children under 14 are underweight or stunted in growth;

— more than 90 percent of the absolute poor are in the rural areas;

— at least 1.43 million blacks in the homelands have no income;

— a quarter of black women in South Africa are separated from their husbands;

— whites who constitute 15 percent of South Africa's population, receive over 70 percent of its income, and 98.1 percent of all income from property accrues to whites;

— only 5.5 percent of South African doctors are in the rural areas where 50 percent of the population live;

— in the homelands there is one doctor per 174,000 people;

— 2.9 million children under 15 suffer from first-degree malnutrition;

— the government spends $913 per capita on education for white children and $140 per capita for black children;

— at least 60 per cent of black teachers are unqualified compared to 3 percent of white teachers.[7]

Provision of housing, and employment for blacks is grossly inadequate. For example, in 1984 in the 'white' areas of South Africa, there were less than 421,000 family housing units available for blacks. 'This means that the average number of black persons per family housing unit ranges from 12 to 24 depending on how it is calculated. The comparable figure for whites is 4 persons per housing unit. . . . In the greater Durban region . . . the Urban Foundation estimated that 1.25 of the 2 million blacks within the functional area live in 'shack settlements'. Living conditions in these areas are extremely cramped, with an average of 10-14 persons per dwelling.[8] It is estimated that in 1985 as many as 3 million blacks out of a potential workforce of 8 million were unemployed.[9]

Pressure for Change

The study above analyses pressure for change in apartheid South Africa coming from outside the country. There is also of course internal pressure. This arises in two interlocking spheres — the political and the economic.

The two most powerful opposition parties are the African National Congress (ANC) and the United Democratic Front (UDF). The ANC was founded in 1912 to fight racial discrimination. For almost 50 years it engaged in a series of peaceful campaigns in defiance of racist laws including civil disobedience, boycotts, strikes and non-cooperation. In 1959 a break-away group, committed to more confrontational methods and considering that white involvement in the ANC was too extensive, formed the Pan-Africanist Congress (PAC).

Both the ANC and PAC announced plans for national campaigns against the pass laws. PAC was to launch its campaign on 21 March 1960. On that day thousands of protestors gathered in Sharpeville to march to police stations and hand in their passes. The police opened fire on them killing 69 people and wounding 180 others. This led to unrest throughout the country. On March 30 the government declared a State of Emergency and arrested over 1,500 activists. Both the ANC and PAC were banned. The ANC then formed a military wing (*Umkhonto we Sizwe*, or Spear of the Nation) and began a campaign of sabotage. After Sharpeville however, most of the senior leadership of the PAC and the ANC were in prison or in exile and resistance to white rule abated. ANC President Nelson Mandela has been in prison since 1964. The Black Consciousness movement emerged in the late 1960s and emphasised self-help and psychological liberation. For a time Black Consciousness filled the vacuum left by the banning of the ANC and PAC.

A new wave of resistance culminated in the Soweto riots of 1976 which began when school children protested against a government decision that Afrikaans be one of the required languages of instruction in black secondary schools. Police opened fire on the students, killing four. During the next 16 months at least 700 people died in clashes with the police. Between June 1976 and September 1977 at least 2,400 people were detained under the security laws.[10] Black Consciousness was one of a number of organisations banned at that time. Its leader, Steve Biko, died in police detention in 1977. In the aftermath of the Soweto riots, over 6,000 young blacks left South Africa many of them going to ANC guerilla training camps in Angola or to the ANC Education Centre in Tanzania.[11]

The United Democratic Front emerged in 1983 as a national multi-racial, umbrella organisation opposed to the new constitution adopted in 1983 and establishing a tricameral parliament with chambers for whites, Asians and coloureds, but not blacks. Despite intense harassment by the government, including widespread detention of UDF leaders and a ban on foreign funding the UDF remains the most important legal opposition

149

political grouping in South Africa. It is very strong at local level and continues to work for 'a single, non-racial unfragmented South Africa — free of Bantustans and Group Areas'.[12]

Other opposition groupings include the Azanian People's Organization (AZAPO) which emerged in 1978 as a successor to Black Consciousness; the Communist Party of South Africa (CPSA) banned since 1950; and Inkatha led by Chief Buthelezi, chief minister of Kwazulu, the government-designated 'homeland' of the Zulus. Inkatha rejects homeland independence and stands for a united nation. It also opposed the 1983 constitution. Inkatha's relations with other opposition groups, particularly the ANC and UDF, are strained not least because of repeated attacks on UDF and black student gatherings. However, with a membership of over 750,000 it retains considerable support in its home area.

Another potent opposition force in South Africa is the independent black trade union movement. Since trade unions were legalised in 1979 as part of the government reform programme they have succeeded in winning improvements in wages and conditions. COSATU, a federation of 36 unions with 600,000 members, was formed in December 1985.

Within the white population too there is opposition to apartheid. The Progressive Federal Party, the most liberal of the predominently white parties, is committed to a gradualist programme of reform of apartheid. A PFP delegation met with the ANC leadership in Lusaka in 1985.

A 60 strong delegation of mainly Afrikaner South Africans had talks with exiled ANC leaders in Dakar, Senegal in July 1987. They discussed '(i) strategies for bringing about fundamental change in South Africa; (ii) the building of national unity; (iii) possible future government structures; and (iv) the economy of a post-apartheid South Africa'.[13]

The business community has also been speaking out against apartheid. This is not least because South Africa is currently experiencing its worst economic crisis since the 1930s. Real economic growth was less than 1% between 1981-85, with per capita GNP falling. Since 1980 the rand has depreciated from $1.28 to less than $.50. Since 1976 there has been only one year (1981) in which South Africa experienced a net inflow of direct private investment.

The link between the economic crisis and the political crisis has been recognised by the business community in South Africa. In its 'Business Charter' for a post-apartheid South Africa published in 1986, the South African Federated Chamber of Industries stated that 'Economic conditions have come to be increasingly dominated by the polarisation of political conditions which directly threaten the stability and prosperity of the country as a whole. In consequence the business community has accepted that far-reaching political reforms have to be demonstrably introduced to normalise the environment in which they do business'.[14] Previously, in September 1985 a group of leading businessmen had travelled to Lusaka in Zambia to have talks with the ANC.

The Current Unrest

In September 1984 a new wave of violence began in the black townships initially in response to rent increases. The situation deteriorated rapidly leading the government to declare a State of Emergency in July 1985 in 36 districts. This was replaced by the nationwide State of Emergency in June 1986, despite opposition from the Asian and Coloured houses of the tricameral parliament.

The current wave of unrest is the most violent and widespread in South Africa this century. Between September 1984 and January 1987, over 2,200 people were killed. Government authority in many townships has collapsed. In the view of the US State Department Report 'there is no longer any prospect that [the Government] will be able to reassert its authority in black areas without sustained repression'.[15]

Prospects for change

A number of factors have led the South African government to embark on a programme of apartheid reforms. First, it is estimated that by the year 2000 the white population of South Africa will be down to 10% of the total. Secondly, since the early 1970s many South African businessmen have recognised that apartheid, by hindering the growth of a skilled and stable black labour force was limiting the scope for further industrial expansion. Thirdly, many influential government advisers argue that blacks have to be brought into government in some way to head off a revolution.

Since 1978, 'the basic thrust of the government's programme . . . has been to reduce some officially mandated racial separation and discrimination without endangering continued white control of the political and economic system or threatening the maintenance of "white identity".'[16] The major reforms to date have been in the areas of labour law including the official recognition of black trade unions; restoration of citizenship but only to less than 2 million of the 9 million blacks who lost their citizenship when the homelands were established, abolition of passbooks and their replacement by a uniform identity card for black and white citizens; establishment of the tricameral parliament for whites, Asians and coloureds, (the proposed National Statutory Council for blacks with only very limited advisory powers has not won the support of any credible black leader); abolition of some forms of petty apartheid e.g. allowing hotels and restaurants to serve all races, permitting racially mixed political parties, allowing mixed marriages.

However, the main bulwarks of apartheid remain. They are the Native Lands Act designating 87% of South Africa's land as 'white' areas, the classification of all South Africans on the basis of race; the homelands policy; and the 1983 constitution excluding blacks from a national political role.

It is the assessment of the US State Department report quoted above, that power rests firmly in the hands of President Botha and his advisers and that the President is in a position to carry the majority of Afrikaners with him. Currently he is moving into a new phase of 'hard-line siege politics'[17] exemplified by the 1986 raids on alleged ANC offices in Botswana, Zambia and Zimbabwe by South African forces, and campaigns to discredit the ANC as potential participants in future negotiations; rejection of the Possible Negotiating Concept developed by the Commonwealth Eminent Persons Group who visited South Africa in 1985; the use of the greatly expanded executive powers given to the President in the 1983 constitution to override parliamentary opposition; the declaration of the State of Emergency; the major restrictions on the press imposed in 1986, etc.

Despite the gains made by anti-apartheid forces such as the new strength of the black trade unions, the emergence of the UDF and the increased recognition of the ANC by the international community and some sectors of white opinion within South Africa as indispensable to any lasting settlement in South Africa, the ending of apartheid is not imminent. Zwelakle Sisulu, the editor of the *New Nation* newspaper who is currently in detention remarked in 1986: 'We are not poised for the immediate transfer of power to the people. The belief that this is so could lead to serious errors and defeats.'[18]

Further Reading

For a more detailed historical analysis of apartheid the reader is referred to the following:

Attwell, Michael, *South Africa: Background to the crisis*, London: Sidgwick & Jackson, 1986
Traces the history of South Africa from before the arrival of the European settlers to the crisis of the 1980's.

Bunting, Brian, *The Rise of the South African Reich*, rev. ed., Harmondsworth: Penguin, 1969 (Reprinted by the International Defence and Aid Fund for Southern Africa in 1986)
Concentrates on the growth of the National Party in the 1930s and 1940s and how it consolidated its power after the 1948 elections.

Cornevin, Marianne, *Apartheid: power and historical falsification*, Paris: UNESCO, 1980
Describes the historical premises on which the ideology of apartheid is based and the myths used to justify it.

Davenport, T. R. H., *South Africa: a modern History*, 3rd ed., London: Macmillan, 1987

A detailed history from the earliest South Africans to 1985:
Part One: The prelude to white domination; Part Two: The consolidation of a white state; Part Three: The political economy of South Africa.

Lipton, Merle, *Capitalism and Apartheid, South Africa 1910–1984*, Aldershot: Gower/ Maurice Temple Smith, 1985
Explores the interaction of racial policies and economic interests in South Africa; examines the pressures for and against apartheid and the changing interests and power of industrialists, farmers, mine workers and white workers.

All of these are available in Trocaire's Library, 169, Booterstown Avenue, Blackrock, Co. Dublin Tel. (01) 885385

References

1 United States Department of State, *A US Policy Towards South Africa*, the Report of the Secretary of State's Advisory Committee on South Africa, January 1987, p.16.

2 Ibid.

3 Ibid., p.17.

4 *Keesings Record of World Events*, London: Longman, Vol. XXXIII, p.35363, September 1987.

5 United States Department of State Report, op. cit.

6 Ibid., p.27.

7 Findings summarised in *Lincoln Letter: X Ray on South Africa*, Lincoln Trust, London and Washington, July 1984.

8 Michael O. Sutcliffe, "The Crisis in South Africa: Material Conditions and the Reformist Response", University of York, Centre for Southern African Studies, Conference Paper for 'The Southern African Economy after Apartheid', 29 September – 2 October, 1986, p.7.

9 Ibid., p.18.

10 United States, Department of State Report, op. cit., p.24.

11 Ibid., p.21.

12 Quoted in United States, Department of State Report, op.cit., p.24.

13 *Keesings Record of World Events*, London: Longman, Vol. XXXIII, p.35362, September 1987.

14 Quoted in United States, Department of State Report, op.cit., p.24.

15 United States, Department of State Report, op. cit., p.26.

16 Ibid., p.18.

17 Ibid., p.22.

18 Ibid.

Bibliography

Books

Aberach, J. A., Putman, R. D., Rockman, B.A. *Bureaucrats and Politicians in Western Democracies*, Cambridge Mass: Harvard University Press, 1981

Carter, G. M. and O'Meara, P. eds. *International Politics in Southern Africa*, Bloomington: Indiana University Press, 1982

Casey, J. *Constitutional Law in Ireland*, London: Sweet and Maxwell, 1987

Catholic Institute for International Relations, *South Africa in the 1980s: State of Emergency*, 3rd ed., London CIIR, 1986

Commonwealth Group of Eminent Persons, *Mission to South Africa — The Commonwealth Report*, Harmondsworth: Penguin, 1986

Europa Publications, *Africa South of the Sahara 1986*, 15th ed., London: Europa Publications, 1985

Forde, M. *Constitutional Law of Ireland*, Dublin: Mercier Press, 1987

Hanlon, J. and Omond, R. *The Sanctions Handbook*, Harmondsworth: Penguin, 1987

Hill, C. *National Foreign Policies and European Political Cooperation*, London: Allen & Unwin, 1983

Holland, M. *An introduction to the European Community in the 1980's*, Cape Town: Juta, 1983

Holsti, K..J. *International Politics*, London: Prentice Hall International, 1972, 2nd ed.

Hufbauer, G. C. and Schott, J. J. *Economic Sanctions in Support of Foreign Policy Goals*, Washington: Institute for International Economics, October 1983

Keatinge, P. *The Formulation of Irish Foreign Policy*, Dublin: Institute of Public Administration, 1973

Keatinge, P. *A Place Among the Nations: Issues of Irish Foreign Policy*, Dublin: Institute of Public Administration, 1978

Keatinge, P. "Ireland: Neutrality inside EPC", in Hill, C. ed. *National Policies and European Political Cooperation*, London: Allen & Unwin, 1983. pp.137-152

Laffan, B. "The Consequences for Irish Foreign Policy" in Coombes, D. ed. *Ireland and the European Communities: Ten years of membership*, Dublin: Gill and Macmillan, 1983, pp.89-119

Lindemann, B. "European Political Cooperation at the UN: a challenge for the Nine" in Allen, D., Rummel, R., Wessels, W. *European Political Cooperation*, London: Butterworth, 1982, pp.110-132

Lipton, Merle, *Sanctions and South Africa: The Dynamics of Economic Isolation*, London: Economist Intelligence Unit, 1988

Macridis, R. C. ed. *Foreign Policy in World Politics*, Englewood Cliffs, N.J., 1968, 3rd ed.

Manseragh, N. *Survey of British Commonwealth Affairs*, London: Oxford University Press, 1952

Moorsom, R. *The Scope For Sanctions: Economic Measures Against South Africa*, London: Catholic Institute for International Relations, 1986

O'Brien, C. C. *States of Ireland*, London: Panther, 1974, revised edition

Orkin, M. *The Struggle and the Future: What Black South Africans Really Think*, Johannesburg: Ravan Press, 1986

Peterson, M. J. *The General Assembly in World Politics*, London: Allen & Unwin, 1986

Razis, V. *The American Connection: The Influences of United States Business on South Africa*, London: Frances Pinter, 1986

Rogers, B. and Bolton, B. *Sanctions Against South Africa: Exploding the Myths*, Manchester: Manchester Free Press, 1981

Sutton, M., *Irish Government Aid to the Third World — Review and Assessment*, Dublin: Trocaire/Irish Commission for Justice and Peace, 1977

Van Praag, N. "European Political Cooperation in Southern Africa" in Allen, D., Rummel, R. Wessels, W. *European Political Cooperation*, London: Butterworths, 1982, pp.134-146

Wallace, W. *Foreign Policy and the Political Process*, London: Macmillan, 1971

_____, "Introduction: cooperation and convergence in European foreign policy" in Hill, C. ed *National Foreign Policies and European Political Cooperation*, London: Allen & Unwin, 1983

Wolfers, A. *Discord and Collaboration: Essays on International Politics*, Baltimore: the John Hopkins Press, 1962

Articles and Papers

Amstrup, N. "The Perennial Problem of Small States: A Survey of Research Efforts", *Cooperation and Conflict* II, 1976:163-182

Austin, D. "A South African Policy: six precepts in search of a diplomacy?", *International Affairs* 62, 1986:391-403

Barber, J. "The EEC Code for South Africa: capitalism as a foreign policy instrument", *World Today* March 1980:79-87

Barber, J. "South Africa: the regional setting", *World Today* January 1986:8-12

Becker, C. M. "Economic Sanctions Against South Africa", *World Politics* 39, 1987: 147-173

Braun, G. and Weiland, H. "Sanctions against South Africa — too few, too late", paper presented to an ECPR Workshop on *Change in South Africa*, Amsterdam, 11-15, April 1987

de St. Jorre, J. "South Africa Embattled". *Foreign Affairs* Vol 65, No. 3, 1987:538

Dolman, A. J. "The Like-Minded Countries and the New International Order: Past, Present and Future Prospects," *Cooperation and Conflict* 14, 1979:57-85

Foot, R. "The European Community's Voting Behaviour at the United Nations General Assembly", *Journal of Common Market Studies* 17, 1979:350-360

Fraser, M., Obasanjo, O. "What to Do About South Africa", *Foreign Affairs* Fall 1986:154-162

Goodison, P. "European Community Member States Aid to SADCC", paper prepared for International Coalition for Development Action (Brussels) Programme on Regional Development Strategies: Focus on Southern Africa, 17 November 1987

Holland, M. (A) "The EEC Code for South Africa: a reassessment", *World Today* January 1985:12-14

_____, (B) "The European Community and South Africa: Economic Reality or Political Rhetoric?" *Political Studies* 33, 1985:399-417

_____, "Three Approaches for Understanding European Political Cooperation: A Case-Study of EC South African Policy", *Journal of Common Market Studies* 25, 1987:295-314

Hurwitz, L. "The EEC and Decolonization: The Voting Behaviour of the Nine in the UN General Assembly", *Political Studies* 24, 1976:435-447

Lijphart, A. "The Analysis of Bloc Voting in the General Assembly: A Critique and a Proposal, *American Political Science Review* 57, 1963:902-917

MacKernan, P. "Ireland and European Political Cooperation", *Irish Studies in International Affairs* 1, 1984:15-26

MacKernan, P. "Irish Foreign Policy: Context and Concerns", *Administration* 35, 1987:172-189

Maull, H. W. "South Africa's Minerals: the Achilles heel of Western economic security", *International Affairs* 62, 1986:671-626

Martin, D., Johnson, P. "Africa: The Old and the Unexpected", America and the World 1984, Foreign Affairs 63, 1985:602-630

van der Ropp, K. F. "South Africa: The Revolution Once More Postponed", *Aussenpolitik* 38, 1987:390-401

Sutcliffe, Michael O. "The Crisis in South Africa: Material Conditions and the Reformist Response", University of York, Centre for South African Studies Conference on "The South African Economy after Apartheid", 24 September — 2 October, 1986, p.7

Unpublished Studies

Mottiar, R. *Economic Relations Between the Major Industrial Countries and South Africa*, May 1983

O'Brien, D. A Study of Ireland's Economic Ties with South Africa, A study prepared for Trocaire 1983

Stewart, J. *Irish Investment Links with South Africa*, A Report prepared for Trocaire, April 1986

Official Documents: Ireland

Assistance to Developing Countries: Annual Reports 1981–1986

Dail Debates Volume 117 (1959) to Volume 376 (1987)

Department of Agriculture: Restriction of Imports of Agricultural Produce from South Africa, Order 1986 (SI no 291 of 1986), 14 August 1986, Pl. 4317

General Assembly, 25 September 1987

Department of Foreign Affairs, Dublin, Ireland's Explanation of Vote, 16 December 1981

————————————, Ireland's Explanation of Vote, 9 December 1982

————————————, Ireland's Explanation of Vote, 5 December 1983

————————————, Ireland's Explanation of Vote, 11 December 1984

————————————, Ireland's Explanation of Vote, 10 November 1986

————————————, Statement by Peter Barry, T.D., Minister for Foreign Affairs, to the United Nations General Assembly, 25 September 1984

Department of Foreign Affairs, Dublin, Statement by Brian Lenihan, T.D., Minister for Foreign Affairs to the United Nations General Assembly, 25 September 1987

Department of Health, Circular on "Contacts with South Africa and the purchase of South African Produce", 4 September 1984

————————————, Circular on "Contacts with South Africa and the purchase of South African Produce", 9 October, 1986

Department of Labour, Speech by Ruairi Quinn, T.D., Minister for Labour and the Public Service to the Annual Delegate Conference of the I.D.A.T.U., 30 March 1986

————————————, Speech by Ruairi Quinn, T.D. Minister for Labour and the Public Service to the Anti-Apartheid Movement, 8 January 1987

Joint Oireachtas Committee on Cooperation with Developing Countries: *Report for 1984*

————————————, *The Bilateral Aid Programme*, 2nd Report, 3 December 1985, Pl. 3695

————————————, *Apartheid and Development in Southern Africa*, 3rd Report, 1986

European Community

Bulletin of the European Communities, 18, No. 11, 1985, pp.144-151. "Code of Conduct for Companies from the EC with Subsidiaries, Branches or Representation in South Africa as revised 19 November 1985 by the Ministers of Foreign Affairs of the Ten Countries of the European Community and Spain and Portugal"

Commission, *The European Community and Southern Africa*, Europe Information, December 1981

_____, *Ten Years of Lome: A Record of EEC-ACP Partnership 1976–1985*, Europe Information, 1985

_____, *Developments in trade with South Africa*, Staff Paper, 7 October 1987

Communique of the Meeting of the Foreign Ministers of the Frontline States and those of the European Community on the political situation in Southern Africa, Lusaka, 3/4 February 1986

European Council: *Statement on South Africa*, 26/27 June 1986, *Bulletin of the European Communities*, 19: No..6, 1986, pp.11-12

European Parliament: *The Steller Report on the Significance of Economic Sanctions*, Working Document 1-83/82, 8 April 1982

_____, *The Scott-Hopkins Report on Southern Africa*, Working Document 1-675/82, 4 October 1982

_____, *Report by the Political Affairs Committee on the political situation in Southern Africa and future prospects*, Working Document 2-58/86/Part I and II, 31 May 1986

_____, *De Backer-Van Ocken Report on the Code of Conduct for Community Companies with Subsidiaries, Branches or Representation in South Africa*, Working Document 2-197/85, 3 January 1986

_____, *Draft Report on the implementation by the Member States of the Community of economic sanctions against the Republic of South Africa*, 7 July 1987

Foreign Ministers: *Statement on Mozambique*, 13 February 1985, *Bulletin of the European Communities*, 18: No. 2, 1985, p.69

_____, *Statement of the Ten on the situation in Southern Africa and South Africa*, 22/23 July 1985, *Bulletin of the European Communities*, 18: No. 7/8, 185, p.104

_____, *Press Release, South Africa*, 10 September 1985, *Bulletin of the European Communities*, 18: No. 9, 1985, pp.76-77

_____, *Statement on South Africa*, 16 September 1986, *Bulletin of the European Communities*, 19: No. 9, 1986, p.83

Official Journal of the European Communities, Information and Notices, Proceedings of the European Parliament in various editions.

Other Documents supplied by Embassies accredited to Ireland

Denmark: Unofficial translation of the Act adopted by the Folketing, 30 May 1986 entitled *Act Prohibiting Trade with the Republic of South Africa and Namibia*

France, Speeches, statements and press releases issued by the French Foreign Ministry on South Africa, 1985-1986

Nordic Council: *Programme of Action against South Africa*, 17-18 October 1985

Norway: Press release on *Norwegian economic boycott against South Africa and Namibia*, undated

Norway: Press release on *New Norwegian measures against South Africa*, undated

Sweden: Translation of the Swedish Government Bill on the *Prohibition of Imports of Agricultural Produce from South Africa*, December 1985

UK: Transcript of a Press Conference given by Mrs. Thatcher at Lancaster House, 5 August 1987

USA: Comprehensive Anti-Apartheid Act of 1986, Public Law 99-440, 2 October 1986

_____, *A US Policy Towards South Africa*, Report of the Secretary of State's Advisory Committee on South Africa, 29 January 1987

United Nations

Everyone's United Nations, New York: UN, June 1986, 10th edition
Year Book of the United Nations, Volume 34, 1980
———————————————, Volume 35, 1981
———————————————, Volume 36, 1982
Index to the proceedings of the General Assembly, 35 Session 1980
———————————————, 36 Session 1981
———————————————, 37 Session 1982
———————————————, 38 Session 1983
———————————————, 39 Session 1984
———————————————, 40 Session 1985
———————————————, 41 Session 1986
UN: Issues Before the 40th General Assembly of the UN 1985–1986, UN Association of the USA, September 1985
UN: Asmal, K. *Irish Opposition to Apartheid*, Department of Political and Security Council Affairs, Notes and Documents, No. 3/71, February 1971
UN: Asmal, K. and L. *Anti-Apartheid Movements in Western Europe*, Department of Political and Security Council Affairs, Notes and Documents No. 4/74, March 1974
UN: *Asmal, K.* Policies of the European Economic Community Towards South Africa, Centre Against Apartheid, Notes and Documents, No. 11/79, May 1979

Note: the National Library of Ireland is the source for all UN documentation and the EC Office, Dublin, for EC publications.

Non-Governmental Organisations

AWEPAA: News Bulletin, No. 8, November 1986
——————, News Bulletin, No. 10, April 1987
——————, News Bulletin, No. 12, June 1987
——————, 'Sanctions Against South Africa: The Importance of a Joint EC Coal Boycott', paper issued in March 1987
——————, 'Imports of South African Coal in EEC Countries, 1982–1986', paper issued in March 1987
——————, D. Joseph Hanlon, 'Sanctions Dossier' for a seminar on support to SADCC and action against Apartheid, European Parliament, May 13-15, 1987
——————, Position Paper on Joint EC Policy on Southern Africa, 7 June 1987
——————, *Southern Africa's Future: Europe's Role*, 1987
Catholic Press and Information Office, Dublin, Press Releases 1986–1987
European Report, European Information Service, Brussels, 1980–1987
Fine Gael: Statements and discussion documents for a number of Ard Fheiseanna
Keesings Record of World Events, Longman, London, 1980–1987
Irish Anti-Apartheid Movement: Annual Reports of Activities and Developments 1971–1987
———————————————, *De Beers in Ireland*, paper presented to an international conference on 'The European Economic Community and South Africa', Dublin, 27-28 January 1979
———————————————, *Irish Policy Towards Apartheid*, submission to the Minister for Foreign Affairs, September 1981
———————————————, The Case for Aid to the Liberation Struggle in Southern Africa, a submission to the Joint Oireachtas Committee on Cooperation with Developing Countries, February 1985
———————————————, Press Releases and Statements on South Africa 1985–1987
Labour Party: *Southern Africa*, Principles of International Policy, paper No. 9, July 1982
Overseas Development Institute: Sanctions and the South African Economy: Briefing Paper, December 1986

Trocaire Position Paper, "Why Third World Aid Should not be Cut", November 1987

Trocaire, Information Pack on South Africa, 1986

Trocaire, Development Cooperation Programme for year ended 28 February 1987

Worker's Party: Press releases and statements on South Africa 1985—1987

Index